# Praise for *Sit Write Share*

In the writer's battle of gremlins versus muses, Kathryn Britton's *Sit Write Share* is filled with well organized, easily doable, and highly adaptable experiments to help you overcome your gremlins, get to know your muses, and write from your authentic inspired voice. *Sit Write Share* is a writer's reference book, a treasure trove, of everything you need to know to take your writing from wavering intentions to reader-ready manuscript. It is a valuable resource for all writers on the road to becoming published authors.

Diana Whitney, PhD
Founder, Corporation for Positive Change
Co-Founder, The Taos Institute
Author of twenty books including *Thriving Women, Thriving World*
and *The Power of Appreciative Inquiry*

I'm gifting this book to every client, colleague, friend, and family member who has ever said, "I have a book in me but I'm too busy to sit down and write it."

Margaret H. Greenberg, MAPP, PCC
Best-selling author of *Profit from the Positive* and *The Business of Race*

*Sit Write Share* offers budding (and established) writers a treasure trove of doable strategies to unlock your writing potential and get your book published. Kathryn writes with wisdom and pragmatism but also understands the deeply emotional and relational aspects of writing. I wish I had Kathryn's insights when I wrote my first book and I will definitely be using them to write my next book.

Dr. Lea Waters, PhD, registered psychologist
Author of *The Strength Switch*

If you have a book in you but you dread writing, *Sit Write Share* will help you turn that around. It has experiments to get past fears, escape writers' block, and view faulty first drafts with appreciation. It can even help you learn to view editing as an act of love for your audience. This book is a resource that every writer should have close at hand. *Sit Write Share* has helped me, and it will help you, too.

David J. Pollay
Best-selling author of *The Law of the Garbage Truck*®

Every writer knows that going from inspiration to written pages is the hardest task we face. That is why Kathryn Britton's guide to help all kinds of writers overcome doubts and distractions so that writing can occur is so brilliant. The exercises prime the pump and get the words going. I've already recommended the book to friends and clients who have a book locked inside of themselves that Kathryn can help them to birth and be proud of.

Caroline Adams Miller, MAPP, executive coach, speaker
Best-selling author of *Creating Your Best Life* and *Getting Grit*

When I wrote my book, I found it was harder than I thought, so I hired Kathryn Britton. She was an amazing writing coach. Without her guidance and nudging, my book would have never been written. I am thrilled that Kathryn has bundled her incredible knowledge and helpful strategies into this fantastic book for every writer to benefit from.

Louisa Jewell, MAPP
Author of *Wire your Brain for Confidence*

If you yearn to express your ideas in writing but are thwarted by the "itty-bitty committee" in your head (see Chapter 1), *Sit Write Share* offers your own writing-coach-in-a-book. As someone who has had the great good fortune to be coached and mentored by Kathryn Britton herself throughout the writing of my own book, I can think of no better gift to the aspiring writer than to have Britton's practical wisdom and clear and encouraging voice at their elbow for those times when their muses fail them. For writers of all stripes, this book is a compelling page turner. I've personally applied many of the ideas and exercises that fill these pages. There's nothing like the feeling of holding your own book in your hands and sending it into the world to make a difference for others. That's both the promise and the reward of *Sit Write Share*. You'll never approach a blank page – paper or digital – the same way again.

Karen Warner Schueler, Executive Coach and President of Tangible Group
Author of *The Sudden Caregiver, A Roadmap for Resilient Caregiving*


From her writing experience, experiments and her own blood, sweat, and writing tears, Kathryn is a true writing Yoda. As the original master says, "do or do not, there is no try"; Kathryn has translated this ethos to writing in this book. I can tell you firsthand that when I follow Kathryn's method and write, yes, my writing is better, but more importantly, my life works better and I am a better person in it. This book is for anyone who is interested in exploring their relationship with writing as a pathway to having more impact in the world.

Jen Grace Baron, co-CEO InspireCorps,
Author of *Dare to Inspire*

I have personally benefited from Kathryn Britton's writing groups for many years. Kathryn has encouraged me and hundreds of others to share powerful stories that we may otherwise have kept to ourselves. With her training in applied positive psychology, Kathryn knows how to tap into positive emotions and mindsets to bring out your best ideas and voice. *Sit Write Share* is a compelling and resource-rich book that gives you access to this brilliance all in one place. If you want to take your writing to the next level, this is the book to read!

Allison Holzer, co-CEO InspireCorps,
Author of *Dare to Inspire*

Whether you want to become a writer for the first time or to stop polishing without publishing, *Sit Write Share* is for you! Using simple and elegant prose, Kathryn Britton offers writers comforting structure: more than 50 practical, creative, experiential writing experiments, and numerous inspiring stories based on her decades of experience as a writer, editor, and coach. *Sit Write Share* will help you defeat your writing demons, design a sustainable, personalized writing practice, and discover joy in sharing and receiving feedback about your writing.

Sherri W. Fisher, MEd, MAPP
Best-selling author of *The Effort Myth: How to Give Your Child
the Three Gifts of Motivation*

Kathryn Britton's book is practical, playful, and profound. She transmits how fun and joyful writing can be, and shares ways to navigate the inevitable frustrations of the writing process. Her 55 experiments liberate and provide structure at the same time, as they invite readers/writers to try out ideas, connect with their strengths, and build productive writing habits to share their unique voices with the world.

Margarita Tarragona, PhD
Director, Instituto Tecnológico Autónomo de México
Center for Well-Being Studies

*Sit Write Share* is much more than three words. Kathryn Britton invites you to take a deep dive to bring your writing potential to life. With practical and structured strategies, she invites you to be deliberately mindful of your imagination and ideas in preparation to write. This process unleashes your capacity to put your ideas on paper, and then compels you to confidently share your words and meaning with others. Kathryn's powerful strategies allowed me to bring out the best in my writing which ultimately brought me great satisfaction and a finished product I am very proud of.

John Yeager
Author of *The Coaching Zone: Next Level Leadership in Coaching*

*Sit Write Share* builds a structure that helps writers overcome the doubts, distractions, and digressions they inevitably face. Written with humor and compassion from Britton's deep experience as an author, editor, publisher, writing teacher, and coach, *Sit Write Share* will make you a better, happier, and more productive writer.

Henry Edwards
Author of *The Daily Better: 365 Reasons for Optimism*

Kathryn's mentorship over the years has had a profound positive impact on my business. Through her workshops, I found my voice and learned how to overcome my fear of failure. Her advice has been critical to helping me consistently produce content that brings in business and it has even led to a book deal with a major publisher. I wholeheartedly recommend this book to anyone who wants to turn their writing from an aspiration into action.

Andrea Goulet, Co-Founder, Corgibytes, LLC and Heartware, LLC
Author of *Empathy-Driven Software Development*

This amazing book should be on the shelf of every writer or aspiring writer across the globe. I believe strongly that the experiments Kathryn details in *Sit Write Share* are the key to making the entire writing process pleasant rather than stressful and judgmental. The experiments in the book are practical and flexible enough to suit every writer's specific needs. If you have been dreaming of writing but have not put pen to paper, look no further. This book will serve as a great guide to making your dream a reality!

Christiana Asantewaa Okyere-Folson, PhD
Author of *Shining Ever Brighter*

Having just written a book, I recognize how little there is out there to help us bring our ideas into the world in a way that makes an impact. *Sit Write Share* is just the book we all need, not only for writing a book, but for any kind of effective written communication.

Homaira Kabir, MAPP, Leadership Development Coach
Author of *Goodbye, Perfect* [March 2023]

Kathryn Britton is one of very few people who has a heart as wide as the world and a wise inner intelligence to match. How wonderful that she combines it all in *Sit Write Share*. This guide to writing will undoubtedly become my trusted companion as I navigate the often rocky terrain of completing my first book. In *Sit Write Share*, Kathryn has found a brilliant way to catalog the challenges and lessons of working with over 125 writers (including me!) from nearly ten years of conducting writing workshops. Not only has she collected dozens of writing experiments to try out, she weaves her loving care through each one. If you have an inclination to write, Kathryn wants you to succeed. *Sit Write Share* is an invaluable tool to help you along your way!

Jan Stanley
Writer, facilitator, celebrant

# Sit
# *Write*
# Share

Practical Writing Strategies to
Transform Your Experience into
Content that Matters

Kathryn Britton

ISBN 979-8-9858246-0-5 (paperback)
ISBN 979-8-9858246-1-2 (eBook)

Library of Congress Control Number: 2022904340

Printed by Theano Press, Chapel Hill, NC, USA

For more information, visit https://sitwriteshare.com

For bulk book orders, use the contact form at the above website.

This book is dedicated to:

*My husband, Edward Glen Britton.*
*May you long be my partner in life's adventures.*

*My children, Laura, Thomas, and Jed.*
*May writing open doors for you.*

*My grandchildren.*
*May your joy in letters on the refrigerator*
*lead to joy in writing.*

# Foreword

A year or so ago, my friend Kathryn Britton told me she was working on a new book project.

The idea grew out of her work as a writing coach and a facilitator of writers' workshops. She had observed the many ways that writers struggle to get from initial idea to polished product, and she had come up with ways to ease those struggles. Now she wanted to share them.

Rather than prescribing solutions, she would present a collection of "experiments," or alternative methods for addressing common problems. Writers could sample from the collection, trying different methods and paying attention to what worked. The book would cover the full scope of the writing process, from getting started to getting published.

It sounded like a perfect distillation of Kathryn's talents. She is not only an accomplished writer and editor; she is also a software engineer. If something she cares about needs fixing, she's inclined to fix it. She's open-minded and non-judgmental. Because of her work in positive psychology, she understands how people change and what makes them thrive.

I was not surprised when, a year or so later, Kathryn told me she had finished a draft of *Sit Write Share*. But when she asked if I would write a foreword to the book, I was taken aback. I had spent a good part of my career teaching courses on writing, but in a very different context. I wasn't sure I could do the book justice.

I was flattered by the request, and our lifelong friendship was a powerful motivator. I asked Kathryn for some reassurance and a deadline. She was generous with both. So, I said yes.

Opening the book to the introduction, I recognized myself in the description of Kathryn's target audience. I am someone who, as she puts it, likes "to have written" but finds writing itself "unpleasant and discouraging." I've always figured that unpleasantness and discouragement go hand in hand with writing: they're the price one pays for getting something written. Kathryn offered a different perspective. Her own relationship with writing had grown into something pleasurable and rewarding.

I encountered myself again in the book's first section, "Sit." Here there is a focus on negative thoughts that keep us from writing in the first place. I nodded as I read about self-doubts and defeatist attitudes, recalling the tenth-grade teacher who pointed out my shortcomings long ago. Several experiments offer ways to tame these thoughts. Others outline strategies for fitting writing into a busy schedule and for making writing sessions less pressured and more pleasant. I realized that I always feel more positive about my writing when I sit at a certain table that faces a window looking out at the street.

The experiments in the second section, "Write," are arranged in three groups: Imagine, Draft, and Edit. A common problem, Kathryn explains, is to try to do these all at once rather than treating them as discrete stages. I am the poster child for this one. I feel compelled to edit as I draft, revising and polishing the initial paragraphs instead of using them as placeholders while I forge ahead to see where the piece is going. The constant revising slows progress and often ends in wasted effort. Kathryn offers ways to avoid this is an experiment called "Draft Without Editing."

In the final section, "Share," I came across another of my stumbling blocks. I really don't like to share my writing until I think it's perfect. But by that point I'm so committed to its final form that I can't bear to change it. This works if the reviewer is a rubber stamp, but not if I need honest feedback. Kathryn's material on seeking and responding to feedback made me realize I was missing out on a chance to improve.

By this point I had fallen under the spell of *Sit Write Share*. I was looking at my problems not as personal failings but as glitches needing a fix. I had tried a few experiments and been encouraged by the results. I knew it would take time and practice to drop old habits, but I could feel stiff muscles beginning to yield. After all, if something you're doing isn't working, there's no reason to keep doing it.

I sat down and wrote my foreword in four words: Read Sit Write Share.

Then I hit Send.

Jane E. Scott

*"It is common sense to take a method and try it. If it fails, admit it frankly and try another. But above all, try something."*

~ Franklin Delano Roosevelt,
   Oglethorpe University address, May 22, 1932

# Table of Contents

Foreword . . . . . . . . . . . . . . . . . . . . . . . . . . . . . . . . . . . . . . . . . . xi

Introduction . . . . . . . . . . . . . . . . . . . . . . . . . . . . . . . . . . . . . .xix

1.  Invitation to Sit Write Share . . . . . . . . . . . . . . . . . . . . . . . . 1

2.  Start With Sit Experiments . . . . . . . . . . . . . . . . . . . . . . . . . 7

3.  Sit Experiments: Act with Intention . . . . . . . . . . . . . . . . . . 9

4.  Sit Experiments: Harness Your Gremlins . . . . . . . . . . . . . . 21

5.  Sit Experiments: Build Habits . . . . . . . . . . . . . . . . . . . . . . 27

6.  Sit Experiments: Spark Inspiration . . . . . . . . . . . . . . . . . . 42

7.  Moving from Sit to Write . . . . . . . . . . . . . . . . . . . . . . . . . 51

8.  Write Experiments: Imagine . . . . . . . . . . . . . . . . . . . . . . . 57

9.  Write Experiments: Draft . . . . . . . . . . . . . . . . . . . . . . . . . 77

10. Write Experiments: Edit . . . . . . . . . . . . . . . . . . . . . . . . . 101

11. Moving from Write to Share . . . . . . . . . . . . . . . . . . . . . . 131

12. Share Experiments: Audience . . . . . . . . . . . . . . . . . . . . . 137

13. Share Experiments: Gather Support . . . . . . . . . . . . . . . . 149

14. Share Experiments: Publish . . . . . . . . . . . . . . . . . . . . . . 165

15. Share Experiments: Network . . . . . . . . . . . . . . . . . . . . . 187

16. Moving From Share Back to Write . . . . . . . . . . . . . . . . . 205

Conclusion . . . . . . . . . . . . . . . . . . . . . . . . . . . . . . . . . . . . 207

Acknowledgments . . . . . . . . . . . . . . . . . . . . . . . . . . . . . . 209

Resources . . . . . . . . . . . . . . . . . . . . . . . . . . . . . . . . . . . . . 211

Credits . . . . . . . . . . . . . . . . . . . . . . . . . . . . . . . . . . . . . . . 212

Selected Publications . . . . . . . . . . . . . . . . . . . . . . . . . . . . 213

About the Author . . . . . . . . . . . . . . . . . . . . . . . . . . . . . . . 215

## LIST OF EXPERIMENTS

Sit Experiment 1:     Read with Intention . . . . . . . . . . . . . . . . . . 10

Sit Experiment 2:     Create Your Own Commonplace Book . . . 13

Sit Experiment 3:     Recall Writing Successes . . . . . . . . . . . . . 16

Sit Experiment 4:     Set an Intention . . . . . . . . . . . . . . . . . . . . 18

Sit Experiment 5:     Face the Voice that Says,
                      "You'll never be a writer.". . . . . . . . . . . . . 22

Sit Experiment 6:     Face the Voice that Says
                      "Who cares what you say?". . . . . . . . . . . . . 24

Sit Experiment 7:     Start a Session with a Reset Ritual . . . . . . 28

Sit Experiment 8:     Build a Tiny Habit . . . . . . . . . . . . . . . . . 31

Sit Experiment 9:     Tie Context to Reward. . . . . . . . . . . . . . . 34

Sit Experiment 10:    Use WOOP . . . . . . . . . . . . . . . . . . . . . . . 37

Sit Experiment 11:    Use Procrastination Aikido. . . . . . . . . . . . 40

Sit Experiment 12:    Cultivate Inspiration Intentionally . . . . . . 44

Sit Experiment 13:    Welcome Constraints . . . . . . . . . . . . . . . . 48

Write Experiment 1:   Decide What Goes In. . . . . . . . . . . . . . . . 58

Write Experiment 2:   Play with Ideas . . . . . . . . . . . . . . . . . . . . 60

Write Experiment 3:   Figure Out Manageable Chunks . . . . . . . 63

Write Experiment 4:   Prime Intuition. . . . . . . . . . . . . . . . . . . . 66

Write Experiment 5:   Collect Story Seeds. . . . . . . . . . . . . . . . . 69

Write Experiment 6:   Mine Stories for Concepts . . . . . . . . . . . 72

Write Experiment 7:   Repurpose Old Writing . . . . . . . . . . . . . 74

Write Experiment 8:   Draft Without Editing. . . . . . . . . . . . . . . 78

Write Experiment 9:   Just Do It . . . . . . . . . . . . . . . . . . . . . . . 80

Write Experiment 10:  Write about Not Being Able to Write . . . . 82

Write Experiment 11:  Write Daily and Keep Records. . . . . . . . . 85

Write Experiment 12:  Work Out Structure of Repeating Units . . 87

Write Experiment 13:  Capture Fleeting Moments . . . . . . . . . . . 91

Write Experiment 14:  Try Speech-to-Text. . . . . . . . . . . . . . . . 94

Write Experiment 15:  Recover in a Hurry . . . . . . . . . . . . . . . . . 96

Write Experiment 16:  End a Session
                      by Planning the Next Session. . . . . . . . . . 98

Write Experiment 17:  Edit in Phases. . . . . . . . . . . . . . . . . . . . 102

Write Experiment 18:   Edit for Content. . . . . . . . . . . . . . . . . . . . . 104
Write Experiment 19:   Cut Mercilessly but Save Your Outtakes . . 107
Write Experiment 20:   Edit for Structure and Order . . . . . . . . . . 109
Write Experiment 21:   Edit Paragraphs and Sentences. . . . . . . . . 112
Write Experiment 22:   Edit Words and Punctuation . . . . . . . . . . 115
Write Experiment 23:   Make Dialogue Clear . . . . . . . . . . . . . . . . 119
Write Experiment 24:   Go Easy on Quotations . . . . . . . . . . . . . . 121
Write Experiment 25:   Include References Deftly. . . . . . . . . . . . . 124
Write Experiment 26:   Read Out Loud to Yourself. . . . . . . . . . . . 128

Share Experiment 1:    Picture Ideal Readers . . . . . . . . . . . . . . . . 138
Share Experiment 2:    Find the Sweet Spot. . . . . . . . . . . . . . . . . . 142
Share Experiment 3:    Check for Cultural Sensitivity . . . . . . . . . 146
Share Experiment 4:    Try Coworking Arrangements . . . . . . . . . 150
Share Experiment 5:    Consider Having a Co-Creator . . . . . . . . 153
Share Experiment 6:    Find a Good Writers' Workshop. . . . . . . . 157
Share Experiment 7:    Run a Writers' Workshop . . . . . . . . . . . . . 159
Share Experiment 8:    Blog . . . . . . . . . . . . . . . . . . . . . . . . . . . . . 166
Share Experiment 9:    Freelance. . . . . . . . . . . . . . . . . . . . . . . . . . 169
Share Experiment 10:   Explore Book Publication Options. . . . . . 174
Share Experiment 11:   Find a Publisher . . . . . . . . . . . . . . . . . . . . 179
Share Experiment 12:   Publish Your Own Book. . . . . . . . . . . . . . 182
Share Experiment 13:   Invite Beta Reviewers . . . . . . . . . . . . . . . . 188
Share Experiment 14:   Establish Your Expertise
                       in Your Author Bio. . . . . . . . . . . . . . . . . . 193
Share Experiment 15:   Gather Social Proof
                       via Endorsements and Reviews. . . . . . . . . 197
Share Experiment 16:   Spread the Word. . . . . . . . . . . . . . . . . . . . 201

## LIST OF INSERTS

Insert 1:   Brian Branagan's Essay on
            Writing and the Five Hindrances . . . . . . . . . . . . . . . . . . 6
Insert 2:   Personal Note Introducing a Commonplace Book . . . . . 13
Insert 3:   An Explanation of Commonplace Books . . . . . . . . . . . . 14
Insert 4:   Elements of the WOOP Framework . . . . . . . . . . . . . . 38
Insert 5:   Five Truths of Inspiration . . . . . . . . . . . . . . . . . . . . . . . 45
Insert 6:   Inspiration Challenge . . . . . . . . . . . . . . . . . . . . . . . . . . 46
Insert 7:   Example of a Repeatable Structure . . . . . . . . . . . . . . . . 88
Insert 8:   Advice on Loss of a File . . . . . . . . . . . . . . . . . . . . . . . . 96
Insert 9:   Cultural Sensitivity Definition . . . . . . . . . . . . . . . . . . 147
Insert 10: Joining a Writers' Workshop . . . . . . . . . . . . . . . . . . . . 159
Insert 11: Publication Activities. . . . . . . . . . . . . . . . . . . . . . . . . . 186
Insert 12: Section from an Email to Beta Readers. . . . . . . . . . . . 191
Insert 13: Sample Endorsement . . . . . . . . . . . . . . . . . . . . . . . . . 198

## LIST OF FIGURES

Figure 1:   Brainstorming with Colored Stickies in Action . . . . . . . 62
Figure 2:   Tracking Spreadsheet . . . . . . . . . . . . . . . . . . . . . . . . . . 65
Figure 3:   A Pomodoro Timer. . . . . . . . . . . . . . . . . . . . . . . . . . . 68
Figure 4:   The Sweet Spot . . . . . . . . . . . . . . . . . . . . . . . . . . . . . 142

## LIST OF TABLES

Table 1:   Collected Morals from the Sit Experiments . . . . . . . . . 52
Table 2:   Stages in a Writing Process. . . . . . . . . . . . . . . . . . . . . 55
Table 3:   My Preferred Reference Approach
           for Online Publications. . . . . . . . . . . . . . . . . . . . . . . 125
Table 4:   My Preferred Reference Approach for Books . . . . . . . 125
Table 5:   Collected Morals from the Write Experiments. . . . . . . 132
Table 6:   Advantages of Publisher and Self-Publish Options . . . 176
Table 7:   Sample Beta Review Questions . . . . . . . . . . . . . . . . . 192
Table 8:   Collected Morals from the Share Experiments. . . . . . . 204

# Introduction

## Do you want to write well and enjoy doing it?

Many people want to have written a book, blog, or article, but find writing unpleasant and discouraging. This book is a collection of ways to move from "I hate writing but I have to do it," to "I find writing absorbing and satisfying." Like playing a sport, riding a bicycle, or driving a car, nobody is born knowing how to write. All of these skills improve with deliberate practice and paying attention. With growing skill often comes heightened enjoyment.

Most of us can remember driving around a parking lot in the early morning hours to learn how to drive a car. After hours of practice, steering became muscle memory, and our feet pressed the correct pedals without conscious thought. Learning to write can also benefit from deliberate practice. By deliberate, I mean practice that leads to experiences of gradual improvement rather than continually recreating writers' block and the harsh self-judgment that makes writing so unpleasant.

I learned this myself, almost by accident. I hated writing in school. Then my high school senior English teacher insisted we write two pieces a week, one in class and one as homework. She returned every piece within a day or two, often with sharp comments. But she also said, "Whee!" just often enough that I really wanted to please her. With her help, I placed out of freshman English in college, but I still had to write papers, and I still found them difficult.

I remember sitting in the graduate library suffering over a five-page paper that just wouldn't come out. In those days, I preferred cleaning toilets to writing papers. But many years of practice later, I suddenly realized that I had learned not just how to get the writing done, but also how to enjoy the process. When I'm writing something now, I feel like a child playing with clay. Who knows what shapes will emerge as I push my thumbs into this plastic medium?

## Think of it as an experiment

Everybody is different. You might find that rising early in the morning to write is just what you need to do, but that would never work for night owls like me. I recommend you enter the space of deliberate writing practice with an experimental mindset, open to trying different approaches in search of the ones that are most productive for you. To aid your search, this book describes a set of experiments for shaping practice. Each experiment might help you write productively. Each experiment has worked for at least some of the writers I've known, but none of them work for all writers.

Perhaps you could dip into the book to find one, two, or three experiments to try initially. Give them a good whirl, perhaps for a few weeks. Then assess how they are working. If they are making writing more enjoyable and productive, celebrate. Maybe add another experiment. Drop any that seem burdensome or heighten self-blame. Feel free to modify any experiment to fit your particular tastes and circumstances. As you proceed, perhaps other experiments will occur to you that were not listed here. By selecting, modifying, and inventing your own experiments, you can move toward a writing practice that fits you.

An early reader acknowledged my suggestion that people dip in and experiment, but she plans to use it differently. Since the book moves chronologically through different writing stages, she plans to use it as a start-to-finish manual for completing particular writing projects.

This is your writing manual to tailor to your own needs.

## Do you recognize yourself here?

Do you need to write to build your business or establish your expertise, but you'd rather do almost anything else?

Do you feel that you have a message to convey that could benefit a much wider circle than the people you meet personally or professionally?

Do you feel that you have been professionally typecast, and you'd like to show people that you have broader expertise?

Does the idea of writing fill you with dread?

Do you keep promising yourself to write, but never quite get around to it?

Do you find writing extremely time-consuming because you erase most of the words that emerge?

If you answered "Yes" to any of these questions, this book can help you.

Let me invite you to write without worrying about whether you are a writer. You are a writer already. You make up new sentences out loud all day long without worrying about whether you are a speaker. Writing is a similar skill that you use daily when you produce emails or texts or grocery lists. All of us could speak more clearly and eloquently by practicing and paying attention. The same goes for writing.

Even seasoned writers face the challenges addressed by this book: to write what they desire, when they want, in the clearest and most eloquent language. It can be a hard job, but you can do it. This book can help you take the next steps, wherever you are with writing skill right now.

## Who am I to lead the way?

I found my own best way to contribute to the world when I started helping other people write. That discovery came after many detours from my English major in college.

I became a computer scientist because programming was fun, and I didn't expect to be doing much writing. To my amazement, I found I spent more time writing English prose than code. My products included specifications, design documents, proposals, and persuasive memos.

Then I became an IBM Master Inventor and helped many people, including my husband, write their first invention disclosures. It made me laugh that some of my colleagues had gotten into computer science to avoid writing papers in college. Even a status update email to the boss needs writing skills.

Like many of you, I didn't start out with a career that taught me to write. I didn't even like to write. I was lucky that practice and good mentors helped me learn to love the activity. Nowadays I shudder when

I hear people say, "I'm just not any good at writing." Nobody was born writing well.

One change in perspective occurred in 2006 when I went back to school to get a Masters of Applied Positive Psychology (MAPP) degree at the University of Pennsylvania. That opened my eyes to effective learning strategies and the ingredients of creativity, persistence, resilience, and optimism. I found I had a gift for writing and helping other people write. Over the past 16 years, I've used this gift to help many writers get the work done.

Along the way, I have been the editor or co-author of several books. I also authored journal papers about positive psychology to add to the papers I wrote as a computer scientist. I wonder, what do people looking at my ResearchGate profile think of my odd collection of interests?

In the last eight years, I have facilitated workshop sessions with more than 125 authors. We have reviewed more than 3000 pieces of writing ranging from short poems to book chapters.

I've seen many ways that people get in their own way. But I have also seen a lot of successful writing happen. This book is my chance to share what I've learned along the way.

# Chapter 1

# Invitation to Sit Write Share

## Why Sit Write Share?

One of my writing clients, Brian Branagan, gave me permission to tell this story. He just wasn't getting words onto the page. In a tone of slight exasperation, I said to him, "Just sit, write, share." Perhaps I was remembering writing papers in college when the only way I could get the first draft done was to make myself sit at a desk whether the words came or not. As Brian and I worked together on various ways to loosen up his voice, he suggested that I turn his new mantra into a book. He inspired more than one of the experiments.

At first, the words seemed like a catchy placeholder for a title meaning roughly, "Plant your butt in a chair until you get the job done, and then let me see what you wrote." But the meaning evolved, as lots of good writing evolves. I shared an early draft of two experiments with a writers' workshop. Participants were enchanted by the working title of the book and saw a much deeper meaning than my initial interpretation. With their help, I could see that each word represented a separate theme that I could use to categorize the experiments.

**Sit**: Many people use Sit as shorthand for meditation and other mindfulness practices. Mindfulness meditation has a lot in common with writing. People experience the same restlessness, inability to focus, and conviction that they are doing it all wrong that afflict people as they write. Some of the same approaches that people use to build a meditation practice also work with building a writing practice. Most of the experiments in the Sit section address awareness and acceptance as well as designing signals to your mind and body that it's time to write and to let go of the nagging belief that you aren't any good at it.

**Write**: Many of these experiments involve ways to unlock, structure, and play with ideas. Other experiments help you capture your ideas in words. A first draft is a major step forward, but not the end of the process. The first draft doesn't have to be either long or perfect. Writing is a multi-pass endeavor. Editing can be an act of love for your readers, as you strive to make your words clear and musical. Writing a first draft benefits from playfulness and tolerance of gaps. Editing benefits from attention to detail. These experiments help you have the right frame of mind for the type of writing you need to do next.

**Share**: Most writing has a social purpose to convey ideas to other people. Even your personal journal conveys ideas to your future self. Yet, writing can seem like a very solitary activity. This category includes experiments that help you involve others in the writing process. Sharing drafts in a writers' workshop is one example. Other experiments help you write to a targeted audience, picturing the people you want to reach and how you want your words to change them. Still others help you set up accountability. People generally keep promises made to others more effectively than ones made to themselves.

When I workshopped the Sit-Write-Share organization described above, one of the readers confessed that she finds meditation quite difficult. She did not find the comparison between writing and meditating helpful. If you feel the same way, just interpret **Sit** as keeping your butt in the chair. But if you have some ease with at least the ideas of meditation, perhaps the comparison will help you notice and allow the distractions without judging yourself harshly. Then you can bring your attention back to the work of capturing your words for others to see.

The experiments in this book are ways to practice the craft of writing. The Sit experiments show how to settle our minds to the task and build habits that return us to writing frequently. The Write experiments show how to imagine what we want to say, draft powerful messages, and then edit rough drafts until they are clear and a pleasure to read. The Share experiments show how to find support from other people and then put words out there for strangers to see.

# Experiment Structure

Some authors decide to create and stick to a particular structure for each unit. When done effectively, the structure helps readers know what to expect. It frees them to focus on the particular points rather than on navigating through them. It also helps readers find their way back to information that they want to use later. I decided to use the following repeated structure for each experiment.

**Story**: A demonstration of someone using the idea in a particular context. Stories make ideas sticky. I gave myself some leeway. Sometimes the story is in two parts with the first part setting up the problem and the second part showing the experiment in action right before the end. Sometimes the story is about the way I came up with the experiment.

**Observations**: Reflection on why this particular experiment works for some people. This section may include references to other resources that readers might find valuable.

**Steps:** A particular sequence of actions to conduct the experiment. In some cases, a step may be very specific, such as "Gather supplies: a timer, a stack of yellow stickies, and a fat-tipped marker," (from Write Experiment 2 in Chapter 8). Other instructions are very open-ended, such as "Read a variety of books, not just books that are similar to the one you want to write," (from Sit Experiment 1 in Chapter 3). Feel free to skip any step or substitute a step that meets your needs more directly. These are not recipes where leaving out the baking powder will make the cake fall.

**Moral**: Many of Aesop's Fables end with a statement such as, "We must make friends in prosperity if we would have their help in adversity." I thought a one-liner would be a cool way to end each experiment. I am using the word moral in the sense of "The moral of the story is," not as a judgment call.

# Story Characters

The stories are composites of real situations that I have observed. With imagination, I have highlighted the relevant points that may not have been obvious at the time. Because they are composites of real and imaginary, I did not want to use the names of real writers that I know except in a few cases when I asked permission. But it is hard to relate to a character named Person X. As I was mulling over that difficulty, I remembered hearing as a child about a family with five members: John, Jane, Jan, Jack, and Judy. Many years later, these names are still in my mind, perhaps because of the musicality of the sequence. I decided to name my characters using names that start with the letter J. If you go by any of these names, I am not calling you out in particular, unless I also include your last name, in which case you said I could.

Because of my own cultural background, I started with names like John, Jane, Jan, Jack, and Judy. Then I tried to branch out to include names that might be culturally more familiar to people from different backgrounds. I hope the names convey a sense of inclusion and my belief that anybody can embark on the adventure of building a writing craft.

## Inserts

Occasionally I include a block of text that I want to set off by itself and reference from other parts of the book. It might be a story written by someone else or a sample email or a summary of a researcher's model.

> I put them in boxes and called them inserts because they are units inserted in the text.

## Resources

Several times throughout the book, I mention this book's resources. I identify the books or papers by scholars whose work underpins the habit experiments in the Sit section of the book. I mention other books that may help you become a better writer or editor in the Write section. I have numerous resources about getting published in the Share section.

Before you get disappointed, these resources are not listed in this book itself for three reasons that I describe in the Resources section at the end of the book. They are instead on a page of my SitWriteShare.com website where I can keep them evergreen as I learn more myself. Whenever I say, "this book's resources," it is an invitation to visit my website.

## Pulling Back the Covers

When this symbol appears, it marks places where I pull back the covers to show actions I took and decisions I made while I was creating this book, including the decision mentioned above about how to handle additional resources. The book certainly changed shape dramatically as I went along. I experimented with different organizational structures, tried out different stories, added and subtracted steps, and tried out different morals.

I also included some of the feedback that I received during my beta review. I sent the book draft to six people who sent me comments. I talk about how I responded to some of their feedback.

I hope my actions and decisions stimulate your thinking about what is right for your writing.

*Insert 1: Brian Branagan's Essay on Writing and the Five Hindrances*

I shared with Rob, my friend and meditation teacher, an essay in which I described the Itty-Bitty Committee in my mind that sounds alarms when I try to write.

"Oh, those are the Five Hindrances," he said matter-of-factly.

"What are the Five Hindrances?" I asked Rob, wondering how he got into my head.

"The Five Hindrances are the mental habits that get in the way of making progress in our meditation practice. They are Restlessness, Sleepiness, Desire, Aversion, and Doubt."

"Yep," I replied. "That's my Itty-Bitty Committee! How do I get rid of them? I can't write when they are chattering in my head."

"Well, Brian, you don't get rid of them. They are always with us but experienced meditators have learned how to continue in their practice and not be stopped by them."

"How do they do that, Rob?"

"You already know how to do it, Brian. You were doing it during our meditation sessions. Do you remember the four ways to handle distracting thoughts?"

It all came back to me. "Sure. Notice, Allow, Ease, Release," I replied. "I notice that it exists. I don't try to make it go away because that only makes it stay in my attention longer. I gently return my focus back to my breath and then, as if by magic, the distraction goes away."

"That's right. You were doing them in the writing you shared with me, too," Rob said.

All those years on the meditation cushion helped me write my essay. I noticed the Hindrances of Doubt and Restlessness. I allowed them by writing about them rather than fighting them. This produced an ease that allowed me to continue (or at least NOT get stopped) with my writing. Finally, I was able to release the essay to others for review.

# Chapter 2

## Start With Sit Experiments

How is a writing practice like a meditation practice? Brian Branagan, the man who urged me to write this book, shows us very clearly in his essay about the five hindrances in Insert 1.

As Brian points out, struggling to suppress the doubts that crowd our minds when we write gives them even more power over us. Instead, we can develop a light touch, acknowledging they are there and then gently moving past them.

The experiments in this part of the book revolve around managing our mental and emotional relationships to writing. There are thirteen experiments in this section. To make them easier to navigate, I have organized them into four categories:

- **Intentions**: Writers can prime themselves for good writing by reading intentionally, recalling earlier writing successes, and setting intentions that guide practice.

- **Gremlins**: Many writers need to face powerful internal voices that pull them down. The voices are often just there and will not go completely away. But it is possible to prevent them from drowning out more creative voices.

- **Habits**: An early reader of this book asked the question, "How do I remember to write?" One solution is by creating habits and rituals. Significant research has clarified how habits are built. I offer ideas and resources to help you apply these findings to build and sustain effective writing habits.

- **Inspiration**: Some people believe they need to wait for inspiration before they can write, and that inspiration is a spark that occurs randomly and burns out quickly. On the contrary, there are explicit actions that writers can take to spark inspiration and keep it going. Surprisingly, working within constraints makes the sparks more likely. Creative people often take steps to establish their own constraints.

I suggest selecting at least one experiment in the Sit section to gather the energy to practice, practice, practice.

# Chapter 3

# Sit Experiments: Act with Intention

*"Wisdom is knowing what should be done next.
Virtue is doing it."*

~ David Starr Jordan, "The Social Order," notes from
an unpublished lecture, in *The Care and Culture of
Men*, 1896

Awareness of intention is a firm basis for taking action. The intention to
write is bolstered by extensive reading and awareness of earlier writing
successes. Writers can also set a direct intention to write for a particular
audience and purpose.

# Sit Experiment 1: Read with Intention

## STORY: READING SHAPES YOUR VOICE

Jolie was writing a memoir that included lots of characters: her parents, her siblings, her teachers, her neighbors, her co-workers, and more. She felt like she needed to describe the individuals coming on her stage. By about the fifth person, her descriptions started sounding alike. Hair color, skin color, eye color, nose shape. Smiling or not. Tall, short, or average.

Jolie asked an experienced editor to review her memoir. The editor suggested she read the beginning of Russell Baker's *Growing Up* to observe the way he introduces people. He describes his mother lying in a hospital bed, always "light-boned" and "delicately structured," but now tiny. His memories of her come in words like "eyes blazing" and "hurled herself at life." The reader can picture her changing from a dynamic force to a shrunken husk.

Jolie went back to her descriptions and tried to focus on the impressions people had left on her, instead of just listing facts about them. Now, her descriptions focused on mannerisms, posture, and voice. What was it like to be around them? What made them unique?

## OBSERVATIONS

In the book, *Writers' Workshops: On the Work of Making Things*, Richard Gabriel says that there are two actions necessary for building writing skill: practicing and paying attention. I heartily endorse both, but I think there are two additional actions that are also fundamental: reading and paying attention while reading.

My mother was a children's librarian. When asked what children should be reading at a particular age, she answered, "Whatever they enjoy reading." She gave one reluctant reader comic books and watched his surprise as he learned that reading could be fun.

Reading was always an adventure in our lives. Even today, nobody in my family goes anywhere without something to read. I am usually in the middle of at least three books. I might be reading a history of India, an explanation of black holes, a popular novel, or a mystery.

With all that reading, I've filled my head with characters that I want to be like or not be like, with language that is beautiful and language that makes me squirm. I've gained a sense of what we humans know and what we don't know yet or maybe can't know. I've seen the wide range that good writing can take, from terse prose to long complex sentences. Reading non-fiction, I have seen cases where the mix of background and fact is just right, and others where the background distracts or the facts are too dry to hold my attention. I've seen what works and what doesn't work for me.

It's wonderful to read for pleasure or information, but it also helps to reflect on what pleases, what illuminates, and what annoys. Reading attentively helps a person develop an ear for language that works. When we write, we make hundreds of decisions about how our words will affect the people who are consuming our material. Those decisions are easier with a built-in language evaluator that comes from lots of reading. Writers who have watched themselves be enlightened, inspired, bored, or confused while reading are better able to understand the needs of their own audiences.

## STEPS

Being mindful of what you're experiencing on your reading journey can make you a more powerful writer. Here are some ideas for reading mindfully:

1. Read a variety of books, not just books that are similar to the one you want to write. Include books that are recognized for clarity and quality as well as ones that catch your fancy. You might find it helpful to read collections of shorter articles by different people, such as annual collections of the best writing on science and nature. You might find a reference list a useful place to start. There are a few examples in this book's resources.

2. My mother was very serious that comic books might be just right for some readers. The right books are often the ones that you enjoy reading. You can learn from both strong writing and writing that is weaker but entertaining.

3. Occasionally stop and ask yourself, "Did that work for me?"

4. Whenever you feel yourself inspired or delighted, observe your pleasure. Where did it come from? Was it the words, the flow of ideas, the twist in the story, the wonder of discovering a new perspective, or something else? Ask yourself, "What can I learn from that?" Consider copying the passage to read again later.

5. Whenever you feel disgusted, bored, or outraged, step back and observe your displeasure. Where did it come from? Was it the clumsiness of the language, the illogic of the argument, the unpleasantness of the viewpoint, the narrowness of vision, or something else? Ask yourself, "Is this something I want to avoid in my own writing?"

6. Recognize that this experiment can last the rest of your life. Reading never stops being beneficial to a writer.

---

**MORAL** Reading develops the mind's eye.

# Sit Experiment 2:
# Create Your Own Commonplace Book

## STORY: THE BOOK OF S

When I was a senior in high school, my English teacher, Ms. Sally Bryan, started me on the path to confident writing. Later we became lifelong friends, so I became comfortable calling her Sally. We wrote each other at least once a year for many decades until she died.

One day, I opened a big envelope from her that contained *The Book of S: A Commonplace Book by Sally Bryan*. It's 32 pages long, ending with a poem she wrote herself. On the back of the front cover, she had taped a piece of paper with this message.

*Insert 2: Personal Note Introducing a Commonplace Book*

> No doubt you are surprised to find this in your mail… but I have been wanting to compile a Book of S, a collection of words others have written that have (in part) shaped me.
>
> This summer, Dori and Kate [her granddaughters] have helped me create a manuscript and then print it out. So here it is! Want it or not!
>
> With love—the true miracle. (And who said that work is love made visible?)

I keep this little book by my desk, opening it when I need inspiration or I can't remember the words of a poem she taught me many years ago.

## OBSERVATIONS

I cannot improve on the words Sally Bryan wrote at the end of *The Book of S*, which are included in Insert 3.

*Insert 3: An Explanation of Commonplace Books*

A commonplace book is an annotated personal anthology—a collection of words and ideas that have changed, enhanced, or broadened the mind of the person who creates the commonplace book. Each commonplace book is unique to the individual who makes it, gathering together anything that has affected the person throughout his or her lifetime.

Commonplace books contain everything from excerpts and poems to song lyrics and cartoons—each item carefully chosen for its personal meaning to the compiler, having touched or interested the person to the extent that words or ideas remain long after the song or book is over. These lingering thoughts and connections are brought together to become a commonplace book.

Commonplace books are not simply an anthology; the thoughts, ideas, and emotions of the collector are reflected in each addition to the book. Authors of poems, quotations, and song lyrics are noted, but the text is often slightly influenced by the compiler, who adds a special touch to each piece in the collection.

A commonplace book can be shared, but the real value is to the person who creates it. That person benefits by taking the time to recognize what they find important and then by creating a record for future reference.

## STEPS

1. Choose a way of collecting information that works for you. Sally's commonplace book was probably a paper notebook in which she copied out words that caught her attention. In our computerized

world, there are other options such as Evernote or online files. As you choose the right tool for collecting your commonplace entries, balance ease against involvement. If it is easy, you may be more likely to continue collecting entries. If you have to work a little to capture an entry, for example writing or typing it out yourself, you might become more involved in thinking about why it matters to you.

2. As you read, watch for words that inspire, puzzle, or intrigue you. Do they change your mind about something? Do they capture deftly something that you've tried awkwardly to explain to someone else? Do you feel changed by reading them? Here are a few examples from my commonplace book. Links to all of these are in this book's resources.

   • The video by George Saunders called *On Story*. I love spending a few minutes with his funny voice and warm wisdom whenever I feel stuck.

   • A passage at the end of Anne Lamott's book, *Bird by Bird*, in which she invites people to think of their truest words as a lighthouse on a hill, shining there to show the way for others.

   • Richard Gabriel's statement that what he calls "risky making" requires skill that can be built with practice and paying attention.

3. If you ever find yourself sending a passage or a link to a friend, perhaps it belongs in your commonplace book.

4. As you capture an entry, record the date. Then you might annotate it with a few words to remind you why it affected you. What was going on in your life?

5. Occasionally flip through your commonplace book to remind yourself of sources that have inspired you or changed your thinking.

---

**MORAL** A commonplace book can be a source of inspiration.

# Sit Experiment 3: Recall Writing Successes

## STORY: REPORTING FROM LEMHI PASS

Jane was blocked trying to write a blog post about something very important to her. She kept starting and then erasing what she'd written. It felt really hard to find just the right words.

What got her unstuck was remembering a time when writing came to her easily and was actually fun.

She was biking the Lewis and Clark Trail from St Louis, Missouri to Astoria, Oregon. Every time she found a library with computer terminals, she'd stop and write up her recent experiences to send in an email to family and friends. Her audience was hungry for her stories about sleeping on the floor of a post office in Montana and braving the scary stretch going downhill from Lemhi Pass. She could tell from their responses that they were thrilled to travel vicariously along with her.

Jane spent some time mulling over what made it so much easier. First, she never had much time so she just wrote what came to mind and figured she could edit it later if she decided to collect her experiences. Second, she had her cloud of friends in mind, so she wrote as if she were telling them her story.

Back to her blog post. She tried writing with her Lewis and Clark audience in mind, typing from beginning to end without stopping to worry about getting it just right.

## OBSERVATIONS

Coaches often use the Stop-Start-Continue framework with clients to help them think about what they want to accomplish and then figure out what they need to stop doing, start doing, and continue doing to get there. Senia Maymin, an executive coach, uses what she calls the ninja version of this framework. She rearranged the order to begin with Continue. She asks her clients what they want to continue doing because it is already going well. She reasons that starting with Continue causes them to remember what has already worked for them, where they are already strong, and where they already have habits or practices that have worked at least once. This helps them realize that they aren't starting from scratch. There is a link to Senia's explanation of the ninja version in the book's resources.

**STEPS**

1. Remember a time when you wrote something that made you proud, whether it was a short email, a letter, or a longer document. Then reflect on the following questions:

   - What helped you get your ideas out?

   - Did you have people who were sounding boards for your ideas?

   - Did you write early in the morning or late at night?

   - Did you create an outline or just start writing?

   - Did you cut and paste from things you'd already written?

   - Did you feel particularly passionate about the topic, or were you a little bit removed from it?

   What other questions could help you to crystalize your memory of past writing successes?

2. Find a way to remind yourself of past successes. Jane posted a picture of herself on her bike at the top of Lemhi Pass above her computer. You might collect comments from readers about what they liked about your writing.

3. Create a mantra that captures what you did that worked so well. Jane's mantra is, "An eager audience awaits." Another mantra might be, "I have an important story to tell."

**MORAL** Extend what already works before worrying about problems.

# Sit Experiment 4: Set an Intention

## STORY: LEAVING A LEGACY

Before starting his book, Jamal stopped to reflect on why he was writing and what he wanted to accomplish. He had been a software executive in three different large corporations. Initially he had been surprised that the same conflicts and issues showed up in all three companies, even though one was a cutting-edge leader and the other two were more mainstream. Then he realized that all were staffed by human beings, with the communication hurdles and complicated motivations that implies.

Jamal felt he had learned a great deal about what worked and what did not. Now two of his children had started in high tech companies. He realized that he wanted to give them and young people like them a head start, rather than leaving them to learn the hard way by making the same mistakes he had made. He imagined them learning from his book how to manage creativity, break down silos, and juggle competing priorities so that they could move up with less pain and confusion than he had suffered. With the intention of helping his children, he was able to get started and keep going even when the writing got complicated.

## OBSERVATIONS

Imagining what you might achieve with your writing is one way to draw yourself to the work. What do you want to achieve? Who will use it? How do you want them to be changed by reading your work? If your purpose includes helping, entertaining, or guiding others, identifying your *why* can move you from self-doubt to excitement as you realize the impact your work can have on others.

Sometimes setting an intention means wading through multiple possibilities. Do you want to contribute to the body of research on a particular subject? Do you want to make research more accessible to people outside academia? Do you want to create a memoir that inspires people or helps them learn from your mistakes? Do multiple topics appeal to you? It's okay to have more than one project open at a time, but sometimes hopping like grasshoppers from topic to topic keeps people from achieving any single intention.

**STEPS**

1.  Take a few moments to consider what you want to achieve by writing. Here's a starting list to select from, but your intention will be much more specific to you. Most of these correspond to the intentions of at least one of my clients.

    •   I want to make the world a better place by helping people flourish.

    •   I have ideas for solving some of our most pressing global problems. I want to find allies and affect the decisions of people in power.

    •   I want to help people avoid mistakes I've made or seen made by sharing what I've learned.

    •   I want to make sense of my own difficult experiences by putting my story into words and then sharing it with others. Perhaps hearing about my struggles will help others face hard times with greater courage and resilience.

    •   I believe I could be a good role model for other people who will face the same challenges that I have already overcome.

    •   I want to create stories for children that help them build skills or understand social issues such as global warming.

    •   I want to write the book that I could not find when I went through a particular challenge.

    •   I want to connect with clients who would benefit from my services.

    •   I want to write fiction that makes people sit up straighter and act more nobly.

2. If you've selected one of the above, adapt it to express your particular goals.

3. If you want to start from scratch, here's a template for a good intention statement: "I want to [action] for [audience] so that [impact]." My statement for this book is, "I want to describe experiments that aspiring authors can use to build writing skills and confidence." My friend, Andrea Goulet, said the statement for her book, *Empathy-Driven Software Development*, might be, "I want to write a reference for software engineers so that they can apply empathy in their daily development practices."

4. Have some fun imagining what your book or article might look like, who might use it, and how they will be changed by it.

5. Review your intention frequently, perhaps each time you sit down to write.

---

**MORAL** Setting an intention can help you step away from doubts.

## Chapter 4

# Sit Experiments: Harness Your Gremlins

Many writers hear unpleasant inner voices that stop words from flowing. It is probably not possible to turn these voices off entirely. It is possible to turn them down so that they do not drown out more creative inner voices.

# Sit Experiment 5:
# Face the Voice that Says, "You'll never be a writer."

## STORY: STOP! MRS. MACGREGOR

I asked Jerry to tell me about the voice in his head that keeps him from writing. After a brief pause, Jerry said, "It's the voice of Mrs. MacGregor, my 10th grade English teacher. I still remember her sniffing when she handed me back an assignment. She said, 'You'll never write for beans. This paper was vacuity of thought wedded to illiteracy of expression.' Whenever I start to write, I look at what comes out and think she was exactly right."

With Mrs. MacGregor looking over his shoulder, Jerry judged every word so harshly that he tended to end a writing session feeling as if he had been in a fight. He'd also have very few words to show for his time.

I invited him to respond differently when he heard her scratchy voice in his head. He could say to himself, "Maybe not then, but I'm getting better all the time. I have work to do. Please leave me alone."

I also reminded him that first drafts do not have to be good. They just have to be the jumping off point for revising until the words become right. There is more on this in the Write section of the book.

## OBSERVATIONS

Writing papers in high school and college did not really help us learn how to get writing done. Howard S. Becker wrote a wonderful book about writing for social scientists. Here's the gist of his description of the experience of writing papers in college: we were more or less coerced to write short essays on topics we knew little about and didn't find very interesting for an audience of one reader who didn't find them very interesting either and only read them because he or she was being paid to do so.

Now we face writing that we really want to do. But we may still be stuck with the feelings and attitudes we picked up writing school papers. The antidote is to remember how things are different:

- We choose our own topics.

- We have gained expertise to back up our writing.

- We can write and then revise, so the first draft doesn't HAVE to be very good.

- Our writing might be read by a lot of people, so we need to keep a broad audience in mind. These are people who can benefit when we share our expertise.

**STEPS**

1. When you find yourself feeling stuck, listen for the critical voice in your head. Can you identify it? Do any memories come to the surface? Notice them without judgment.

2. Reflect on the various skills that you use almost without thinking. Possible examples include riding a bicycle, sewing a seam, using a smartphone, and driving a car. Which one brings the clearest memories of starting something you did not know how to do? Think about the specific actions that helped you gain expertise. Remember missteps as well as triumphs. Use that to help you work through self-doubt and writing resistance.

3. Create your own personal mantra to remember that you are on the way to better writing and that your output does not have to be perfect to move you forward. An example might be, "Celebrate shitty first drafts."

**MORAL**  Nobody was born writing well, but many learn with practice.

# Sit Experiment 6:
# Face the Voice that Says, "Who cares what you say?"

## STORY: SOMEBODY NEEDS YOUR WORDS

After years as a personal trainer and exercise group leader, Jacinta decided to write a book about getting in shape. She wanted to describe what she found worked best among her clients. She had helped many people overcome long-time aversion to exercise and build lasting fitness habits. She believed in incorporating elements of fun, humor, music, dance, and social connection. She also believed that no approach works for everybody, so she watched for things that lit her clients up.

Every time Jacinta sat down to write, she heard voices in her head saying things like,

"There are already thousands of books out there on exercise. Why would the world need another?"

"Who are you to write this book? There are surely people out there with more education, more experience, more knowledge than you have."

The voices all came down to, "Who cares what you have to say?" They were so loud she felt completely stifled.

A friend reminded her that she didn't even like the books written by the top figures in her field. She had a different approach. She remembered the good outcomes she had with clients facing major challenges. Perhaps her approach was exactly what some people needed.

## OBSERVATIONS

Humility is generally a good thing. It keeps us from assuming the world revolves around us. It is worth considering two real and important questions before investing heavily in writing.

**Question 1:** Do I have something to contribute, or will I just be diluting what is already there?

It is highly unlikely that anybody's message will be completely unique. There are lots of people writing now, and there are more pathways to publication than ever before. But that doesn't mean Jacinta's writing is a waste of time. The world needs important messages to be reinforced with different stories. Jacinta's approach may resonate with people who've been uninspired by other books about fitness. Her style, her whacky sense of humor, her specific experiences, and the sequence of exercises she creates may be just what many people need to get up and move.

**Question 2:** Do I have the skill and knowledge to add to what's already written?

Before answering this question, let's consider the Dunning-Kruger effect. This is the name of a cognitive bias about self-evaluation that showed up in studies of undergraduates completing a test of their knowledge of standard written English. After the test, they rated their own ability. The bias was this: the students scoring the lowest tended to *overestimate* their grammar ability by a lot. In contrast, those who scored highest tended to *underestimate* their ability. The conclusion was that humans are not very good at estimating their own abilities.

Many worried writers underestimate their knowledge and ability. If you are plagued with doubt, it may be helpful to talk to others to better calibrate your self-judgments.

---

**STEPS**

---

1. When you find yourself saying, "Who cares what I say?" acknowledge that it is a good question that is worth consideration. Whenever you invest time or money, it's worth evaluating potential outcomes. What difference can your writing make to you and to others? Here are a few options to prime the pump as you think this through:

   - Demonstrate your expertise, thus opening new opportunities.

   - Reach people who are left unmoved by other publications.

   - Adjust a conventional message for a specific audience. For example, Jacinta's audience is primarily inner-city mothers who have neither time to attend gyms nor access to good places to be outside.

- Soften hearts that are normally hardened toward a particular topic. Remember that people don't respond to generalities the way they respond to individual stories.

2. Write a paragraph about what makes you the right person to write on this topic. What experiences, expertise, training, beliefs, or values make you worth listening to? If you are writing a book, this paragraph may become an About the Author section. In the meantime, write it on a card to pull out when you hear this question in your mind again.

3. Get feedback from other people. Perhaps try writing an article or a book chapter about your chosen topic in the style you intend to use. Then find a way to get opinions from people who represent your intended audience as closely as possible. Don't just ask your friends, though their input may also be helpful. Ask people who would be willing to tell you whether they'd buy your book or not and whether they'd recommend it to their friends or not.

4. As we'll discuss in Share Experiment 7 in Chapter 13, be sure to ask people about what they like as well as what they don't. If you plan to alter your approach based on what you hear, collect information about what NOT to change as well as what to change.

5. If feedback tells you that you're on the right track, capture some of the complimentary comments in places that you can return to when that critical voice in your head starts chattering.

### STORY CONTINUED

Yes, Jacinta finished her book.

**MORAL** Your voice may be just what someone needs to hear.

Chapter 5

# Sit Experiments: Build Habits

*"…habit simplifies the movements required to*
*achieve a given result, makes them more accurate*
*and diminishes fatigue."*
~ William James, *The Principles of Psychology*

Writing gets done one session at a time. If it's hard to remember to write or if every writing session is hard to start, it is difficult to put in enough time. That's where habits come to the rescue. It is also possible to manage motivation to gain energy to proceed.

# Sit Experiment 7:
# Start a Session with a Reset Ritual

## STORY: DISTRACTED BY WHAT WENT BEFORE

Janice sat down to write a blog post that she really wanted to get done this week. But her head was spinning full of details about the meeting she just had at work. Had she said the right thing? Had the people in the meeting understood her? Would they pay attention to the suggestions she made? Had she asked for enough feedback? Was there anybody there that would sabotage her idea?

Then came the grocery list. Had she remembered everything she needed for the cake she intended to bake for her husband's birthday? Then came the gift she had bought him. Would he like it?

## OBSERVATIONS

What often works here is to have a personal ritual for acknowledging all the thoughts spinning through our heads, asking them to step aside for the moment, and creating space for our brains to focus on the task at hand. Having a *reset ritual* like this can be helpful for any transition from one activity to another. For writing, an activity that we don't always enjoy when we first start, it can make a huge difference.

I go through certain steps to get my grandson ready for a nap. I put on his sleep sack, read him a certain story, and then rock him while singing certain songs. All of these actions are signals to him that it is time to let go and sleep. Perhaps you too have a ritual for letting go of the day when you're ready to sleep.

Similar series of actions can signal to our whole bodies that it's time to write, once we've practiced it enough times.

**STEPS**

1. Pick actions to perform to signal to your body and mind that it's time to write. Your ritual might have one step or several. Here are some potential ingredients for your ritual:

   • A physical stretch

   • A bathroom break in which you comb your hair and brush your teeth

   • A walk to the breakroom to fill your coffee cup

   • Closing your door and switching off your phone

   • Sitting in a particular place with supplies at hand

   • Lighting a candle

   • Putting on background music

   • Closing all the windows on your computer except the one open for writing

2. Carry out your ritual every time you sit down to write. You are building up an association between your actions and your intention.

3. View your ritual formation with an air of experimentation. After a few days, if your ritual seems too time-consuming or clunky, streamline it. If you go a week or two without feeling any sense of being prepared, try adding or deleting an ingredient.

4. Persist. It may take a number of times before the actions become a signal to your entire self to focus attention on allowing words to flow out of your fingers onto the page.

## EXAMPLE

Here's a reset ritual to try. I adapted this from the exercise on day 22 of my friend Jane S. Anderson's book, *30 Days of Character Strengths*.

1. Pause and feel inbreath and outbreath for eight breaths. Let everything go except for breathing. Give your breath your full attention.

2. Conclude with a question: Which of my positive qualities might I bring forward right now?

3. Reflect on that positive quality. Imagine using it to move your writing forward. Perhaps you find yourself thinking of **Curiosity,** inspiring you to be open to what comes up when you focus. Perhaps **Leadership** causes you to work on defining a direction so clearly that others will want to follow. Perhaps **Hope** will move you to write about a future that is better than the present for individuals, groups, or societies.

4. Turn your attention to the page. Let your positive quality help words emerge.

**MORAL** Clear your brain for writing by putting away what went before.

# Sit Experiment 8: Build a Tiny Habit

## STORY: ONE SMALL STEP FORWARD

Sharon Danzger wanted to start a meditation practice. She knew there were so many benefits. She had read that she should start with 10-20 minutes a day. For someone who had trouble sitting still, that seemed impossible.

Finally, she asked herself, "What is the smallest amount of time that I can commit to each day? At the end of the day, I don't want to say, 'This is important, but I didn't have the time.'"

The answer came back, "I can commit to two minutes."

She sat with a kitchen timer and meditated for two minutes every day, focusing on her breath. Some days it went quickly. Other days it felt very long. At times when she felt like jumping out of her skin, she reminded herself that it was only two minutes. "If I can't sit comfortably for two minutes, perhaps I need this even more than I thought!"

Eventually she found a free meditation app. Once she began using guided meditations, the sitting became easier, and she gradually increased the time. After a few months she had worked up to 10 minutes. She continues to meditate for 10 to 15 minutes every day.

## OBSERVATIONS

In his book, *Tiny Habits*, BJ Fogg explains that it is hard to make new habits by relying on will power and motivation. This is particularly hard when ability is low, as it generally is when we start a new behavior. Whether that's doing pushups, learning a new language, or writing, it takes a lot of motivation to get us moving, and that motivation is hard to sustain.

Fogg suggests celebrating changes in the right direction, no matter how tiny they are. Tiny changes do not require lots of ability. Even somebody with a low level of ability could do one pushup, or at least a pushup against the wall. After tiny changes, it is important to reward ourselves, thus intentionally using our internal neurochemical reward system to wire in changes. Tiny steps can eventually make deliberate actions turn into automatic habits.

By tiny, he means tiny. In an experiment with people who wanted to form a habit of flossing their teeth daily, he found that the group that committed to flossing one tooth daily were more likely to build a regular flossing habit than people who committed to flossing all their teeth.

## STEPS

1. Decide what constitutes the tiny behavior that you want to grow into a habit. Is it writing two sentences? Writing for five minutes? This is your personal equivalent to flossing one tooth.

2. Select an anchor moment. This could be something that you're already doing habitually, such as eating breakfast, filling your coffee cup, getting dressed, or walking the dog.

3. Every day, perform the tiny writing behavior immediately after the anchor moment.

4. Reward yourself for completing your tiny writing behavior. For example, smile at yourself in the mirror or tell yourself, "You did a good job," or do something fun for a few minutes.

5. If you are moved to go beyond your tiny writing behavior, for example writing for 10 minutes, that's great. But remember it is extra credit.

## ANOTHER STORY:

Reflecting on her own writing history, Jane S. Anderson concluded, "A better approach, for me at least, was to establish a habit of writing. I started by carving out a little bit of time each day, literally starting with five minutes and gradually increasing the time until I was writing daily for at least an hour and often longer. By writing regularly, I began to hear my voice, allow my thoughts to percolate, and create new content as well as edit old."

MORAL  Simple steps change behavior.

# Sit Experiment 9: Tie Context to Reward

## STORY: WORKING THE HABIT SYSTEM

Jeb wasn't getting the writing done that he really wanted to do. Every day, he went to bed thinking, "Where did the time go? I know I deeply want to write this book. What is the matter with me that I don't get it done?" Like many people observing himself failing day after day to do something he really wanted to get done, he believed that he was low on will power. The self-blame accumulated, but it did not change his behavior.

A friend suggested that he focus instead on building a writing habit. The friend pointed out that Jeb habitually brushed his teeth, worked out, and called his mother daily. All of these behaviors required effort, but none of them required him to exercise will power. He was just used to doing them. Get up, brush teeth. Finish work, go running. Finish dinner, call Mom. Get ready for bed, brush teeth again.

Jeb decided he would write every day for 30 minutes right after lunch. He packed his own lunch in a lunch box that he had been using since he started work. At first, he put a card in his lunch box that said, "Go write," to remind him of his resolution. He liked to write first drafts in long hand, so he put a legal pad with a ball point pen in the same bag with his lunch box. He also included a few pieces of his favorite chocolate to eat while he wrote. After a few weeks of intentionally picking up the pen, it became automatic. Finish lunch, start writing. The pages started to accumulate in his writing folder.

## OBSERVATIONS

Wendy Wood, another researcher on habits, is a firm believer that the unconscious habit system is a learning system that can be trained. The training takes conscious effort, but once the habit system kicks in, behaviors can be maintained without the expenditure of will power. Will power is a scarce resource for all of us.

Training the habit system involves intentionally creating associations between context and behavior. These associations occur when we perform the same activity in the same context over and over and when we accompany the behavior with something that feels like a reward. Wood explains that the reward stimulates dopamine production, and dopamine strengthens the mental links between the behavior and the context. She also suggests removing friction, the obstacles in the context that make performing the habit harder. Practicing with reward and removing friction is her recipe for habit formation.

Let's look at Jeb's story. He chose a context for his writing behavior. Then he repeated the behavior multiple times in the same context with the addition of the chocolate that served as a reward. In his brain, his habit system started associating closing his lunch box with starting to write. He kept his eyes open for distractions that kept him from completing his work. For example, he found it helpful to silence his phone and tuck it in his lunch box until after his writing period ended.

## STEPS

1. [Skip over this step if it makes you feel discouraged.] Start by reflecting on other habits you have successfully formed. Brushing your teeth? Showering before work? Picking up the mail? Hugging your children? This reflection will remind you that you've trained your habit system before, intentionally or not. What worked best for you?

2. Decide on the behavior you want to make a habit. Do you want to write for 30 minutes every weekday? Write for longer periods on weekends? Write during the workday whenever you are not specifically meeting with somebody else?

3. Decide on the context that you want to stimulate writing behavior. Context could be place, time, other activity, signal, or some combination. As you consider context, make sure it happens often enough that you perform your writing at the desired frequency.

4. Decide on something that your unconscious mind will consider a reward. It could be food, music, or letting yourself do something fun that you only let yourself do during periodic breaks in the writing.

5. Use whatever reminders you need to perform your behavior intentionally and repetitively until the habit forms. The number of times required depends on the complexity of the habit. It also depends on the individual. There's no fixed number of times that work for everybody and every habit.

6. As you practice, watch for things that get in the way. Wood also suggests that habits form better when we remove friction from the habit system. Do telephone calls distract you from writing? Consider turning off your phone during writing periods. Do other activities on your computer lure you away from writing? Consider closing all windows except the one in which you are writing.

7. This may be an area where working with a coach who can help you tailor the habit recipe to your specific needs would be helpful.

8. True success is when you sit down to write regularly as a matter of course with little will power required. Along the way, you may want to observe and reward yourself for desired benchmarks. This could include times practiced, minutes spent writing, words produced, or something else.

---

**MORAL** Use context and rewards to train your brain's habit system.

# Sit Experiment 10: Use WOOP

Jared had been working for years on various writing projects and kept getting sidetracked by other opportunities. One day, he made a resolution to finish one writing project. Sorting through his options, he laid aside writing blog posts that might build his career because that felt unexciting. He decided against working on the memoir that his family had been urging him to complete. They wanted to have it more than he wanted to write it. Politics had completely absorbed him, and he had many things to say about the ups-and-downs of his party. Therefore, he settled on writing about his political activism over the previous election cycle.

At the suggestion of a coach, Jared wrote a one-sentence intention statement that he posted by his computer. He did this by first imagining people reading his writing and then thinking about how he wanted to change them. The coach also suggested that he think about the ways he might get sidetracked and write out his planned responses. These statements acknowledged the obstacles he might face and helped him plan ways to dodge them.

Jared wrote down, "I will make a list of the stories that I want to tell. If I sit down to write and my mind is blank, then I will look on my list of stories yet to be written and pick one." He also wrote, "If I start writing and my words look dumb, I'll remind myself that first drafts are only the first step along the way to good writing."

## OBSERVATIONS

This experiment is based on Gabrielle Oettingen's WOOP framework summarized in Insert 4.

*Insert 4: Elements of the WOOP Framework*

W = Wish: state the goal you wish to achieve.

O = Outcome: imagine in detail what the outcome of achieving the wish might be.

O = Obstacle: identify the obstacles that will keep you from achieving the outcome.

P = Plan: figure out what you will do to get past the obstacles.

This approach has helped many people make progress building new habits and achieving important goals. Oettingen has found that it's not enough to picture the outcome thoroughly. People also need to be aware of the obstacles that they are likely to encounter and create plans to face them. These plans generally take the form, "If [Obstacle] happens, then I will do [Response]." Jared, for example, might say, "If I start worrying about something else while I am writing, I will write my worry on a post-it note and put it where I will see it when I am finished." There are links to more WOOP information in this book's resources.

## STEPS

1. To accomplish the first two steps of the WOOP approach, stating your goal and picturing the outcome, take some time to imagine in as much detail as possible what you want to achieve and what it will be like to achieve it. This might be a time to revisit your intention statement if you did Sit Experiment 4 in Chapter 3.

2. To identify obstacles, observe yourself over a week or two. Here are possible obstacles.

   - Do you spend all your time figuring out what to write?

   - Do you erase your words as soon as you write them?

   - Do you get distracted easily?

3. Once you know your personal obstacles, plan the actions that will help you get past them.

---

**MORAL** Become aware of obstacles so you can move around them.

# Sit Experiment 11: Use Procrastination Aikido

## STORY: MANAGE MULTIPLE MOTIVATIONS

This a story about me and something I noticed when I was in college. When I got a reading assignment that I didn't find interesting, such as Emmanuel Kant, I'd find ingenious ways to avoid reading. I dreaded the effort to keep myself sitting in a chair with the book open in front of me. That continued until I had a paper assigned. Then it became much easier to focus on Kant, because writing papers was even less appealing. Papers became easier to write when exams were scheduled. Perhaps I worried too much about whether I'd review the right things, and I dreaded the anticipated time crunch of the final exam. In fact, when exams were scheduled, I preferred cleaning the oven and scrubbing the toilet to rereading all my notes.

## OBSERVATIONS

Nobody is equally motivated by everything they need to do. It is possible to use these differences in motivation to unlock energy for difficult tasks. I used to call this my procrastination hierarchy, but now I think of it as Procrastination Aikido because it involves redirecting energy from avoiding a less desirable task toward getting writing done. I learned to manipulate this energy deliberately. If I found myself stalling on something I really needed to get done, I'd make myself think of something I wanted to do even less. That almost always got me going.

I know I am not alone operating this way. The wife of one of my friends said that she can always tell when he needs to write something because the items on his honey-do list start getting done. Look at your to-do list as a whole, not one item at a time.

### STEPS

1. Make a list of the things you need to get done

2. Rank them from least appealing to most appealing

3. Notice where writing appears on the list

4. Focus on something less appealing than writing. Use that avoidance energy to motivate yourself to write by saying to yourself, "If I don't write, then I need to go [fill in the blank]." Work on taxes? Ream out the basement pipe? Take stuff to the dump? Name whatever it is that you least want to do.

5. If you have something really appealing on your list, tell yourself, "I'm going to write for an hour and then I'll let myself [fill in the blank with appealing activity]."

6. If your entire to-do list is more appealing than writing, imagine facing the consequences of not writing. Who will you have to tell? How will they respond to you?

7. If even that task is more appealing than writing, perhaps this is not the experiment for you. Perhaps you also need to look at whether writing belongs on your list at all, unless avoiding it really helps you get something else important done.

———————— // ————————

I can almost always find something I want to do even less than writing, but sometimes avoidance of writing helps me get something else done.

---

**MORAL**  Let avoiding one task motivate you to do another.

Chapter 6

# Sit Experiments: Spark Inspiration

*"Inspiration can be actively sought after and sustained over time."*

~ Jen Grace Baron, Allison Holzer, Sandy Spataro,
*Dare to Inspire: Sustain the Fire of Inspiration in Work and Life*

It is not necessary to wait passively for inspiration to occur. You can find your own best ways to get and stay inspired. Constraints can open the door to creativity.

# Sit Experiment 12:
# Cultivate Inspiration Intentionally

## STORY: NO MORE ABRACADABRA

Jasmine had a complicated ritual for starting a writing session. She thought of it as sending a request to the universe. There were many steps, including completely clearing her desk, breathing deeply a certain number of times, lighting a candle, and putting on just the right music. Then she would sit waiting for inspiration. When it arrived, she scribbled furiously for fear it would leave her. When it did not arrive, she would think, "Well, I wasn't meant to write today."

One of her good friends gave her a copy of *Dare to Inspire*, a book that challenges the idea that inspiration is fleeting and out of our control. Jasmine read it with interest, marking the actions that she intended to try right away. She eventually stopped picturing inspiration as random flashes of brilliance that burn out swiftly. She started recognizing her own ability to call up inspiration, direct it toward her writing, and keep it burning brightly while she worked. Jasmine developed an intentional practice that helped her spark, stoke, and direct inspiration.

## OBSERVATIONS

This experiment is based on *Dare to Inspire* by Allison Holzer, Sandra Spataro, and Jen Grace Baron. It is only a quick taste of their approach.

Sparks of inspiration come from the intersection of possibility and invincibility. Think of possibility as an openness to seeing things in new ways. Invincibility is a confident energy that turns possibility into action. Intentional practices can keep the sparks of inspiration from flaming out.

Insert 5 summarizes the five truths of inspiration that are described in the book. Each truth is accompanied by specific actions to put it into practice.

*Insert 5: Five Truths of Inspiration*

1. Inspiration is highly personal and evolves over time.

2. We have agency and choice about inspiration in our own lives.

3. There are reliable engines that spark inspiration.

4. Inspiration can be sustained over time.

5. Inspiration is contagious.

**STEPS**

Below are some ideas directly inspired by the book, *Dare to Inspire*.

1. **Possibility**: Think about your purpose for writing. Whom do you want to reach? How do you want your words to change them? Widen your aperture slightly. Imagine reaching a broader set of people. Picture having a more powerful impact. Write down your expanded purpose. Read it whenever you start writing. Whenever it feels stale, try widening your aperture even further.

2. **Invincibility**: Draw on your own past successes. Bring a particular success to mind. What gave you the confidence to act? What gave you the courage to do things you'd never done before? What sustained your hope that you could have the impact you envisioned? Think about ways to apply your confidence, courage, and hope to this writing project.

3. **Engines of Inspiration**: Use the InspireCorps worksheet shown in Insert 6 to evaluate how much you use each of the eighteen inspiration engines described in their book.

   • Pick one that you already use relatively frequently. Consider how you could use it more often.

- Pick one that you hardly ever use. Consider how you could introduce it into your writing practice.

4. Contagion: Do you have a writing partner that would be willing to explore inspiration with you? Perhaps you could find ways to help each other keep the fire burning.

---

**MORAL** Find your muse inside yourself.

*Insert 6: Inspiration Challenge*

| INSPIRATION CHALLENGE |
|---|
| Using this worksheet, review all eighteen engines. |
| 1. Rate each on a scale of 1 to 5 in terms of how much this engine is a current source of inspiration for you. 1 is hardly at all. 5 is very frequently. |
| 2. Circle your top three. These are your inspiration fingerprint – or your unique combination of go-to engines you rely on. |
| 3. Now pick one engine you've never considered before: |
| • What would it look like to intentionally activate this engine of inspiration this week? |
| • What could you do or think about differently to try out this engine? |

| Engine of Inspiration | How much do you use it? |
|---|---|
| Connecting to & Voicing Values and Purpose | |
| Using Your Strengths | |
| Progressing Toward & Achieving Success | |
| Using Your Whole Brain with Unstructured Time | |
| Developing New Perspectives | |
| Activating Body Movement and Presence | |
| Belonging | |
| Admiring Our Mentors and Heroes | |
| Getting a Lift | |
| Serving Others | |
| Sharing a Group Mission | |
| Being Vulnerable & Transparent | |
| Seeking Environments that Move Us | |
| Overcoming Constraints | |
| Witnessing Excellence | |
| Using Your Unique Passions to Make a Difference | |
| Sharing Experiences with Large Groups of People | |
| Experiencing Grief, Loss, or Failure | |

Used with permission from the authors of *Dare to Inspire*.

# Sit Experiment 13: Welcome Constraints

## STORY: EMBRACE THE SHAKE

I cannot think of a better illustration for this experiment than the TED2013 talk by artist Phil Hansen. I highly recommend spending 11 minutes with him. He tells a great story, and his artwork is amazing. The link is in the resources for this book.

Just in case you do not want to put the book down to go view his video immediately, here's the story in brief.

Phil Hansen is an artist. In art school, he created pictures by making tiny dots that together merged into clear images from a distance. After some time, his hand started to shake uncontrollably so that he could no longer draw dots. The marks looked more like tadpoles. His hand hurt. This seemed like the end of his dream of being an artist.

He consulted a neurologist, who told him the damage to the nerves in his hand was permanent. The neurologist went on to suggest, "Embrace the shake." Phil did, with incredible results. He used unconventional materials that allowed him to let go of imperfections, sometimes in dramatic ways. Those words could be a rallying cry for all of us when we encounter constraints that seem to block the way forward. What art could he make with shaky hands?

Phil got a job. With his first paycheck, he went to the art store and bought all the supplies he had not been able to afford in art school, everything he thought an artist could possibly need. With all those materials and tools to choose from, he found himself creatively blank.

He went through a process that proved frustrating at first, but then, liberating. Phil restored creativity by imposing constraints on himself. For example, what could he create with only a dollar's worth of supplies? What could he create with frozen wine or matchsticks? When he imposed constraints on himself, his creativity blossomed. "Looking at limitations as a source of creativity changed the course of my life," he says.

His artwork really is amazing.

## OBSERVATIONS

I am really tired of "Think outside the box." People throw this statement around as a recipe for creativity, but maybe that is backwards. What if instead we think of ideas being like molecules of gas? If they are kept in a box, they exert pressure against the sides of the box, pressure that is creativity. If they are let loose, they disperse, and the pressure drops.

Constraints reduce the need to think about irrelevancies that drain creativity without moving you forward. For example, many poets over the centuries have found writing sonnets, a highly constrained structure, a great opportunity for creativity. They didn't waste their time thinking, "How many lines? What rhyme scheme?" Scientific research papers all tend to have the same basic structure but can vary widely in terms of clarity and importance. The scientist did not have to invent a new structure to present results.

As Phil Hansen suggests, you can even be creative in the design of your constraints. As an experiment, try out various sorts of boxes to see which ones spark your own creativity.

## STEPS

1.  Look for the constraints that already exist for the writing you want to do. Instead of resenting the constraints, embrace them. Examples include:

    - Word limit

    - Assigned outline

    - Required structure

2. Figure out constraints you could impose on yourself. Examples include:

- Allowing only a small percentage of your sentences to be complex or compound.

- Including no more than three items in any list.

- Telling a story entirely from one person's point of view without any all-knowing narration.

- Avoiding words with more than two syllables, a particularly useful constraint when writing children's books.

- Writing for a 7th grade level using one of the readability formulas measured by various online tools. Some of these tools are listed in the book's resources.

3. Experiment with a particular constraint. Don't give up on it too quickly. It may take time to get past the initial discomfort.

---

**MORAL**   Constraints may be advantages in disguise.

# Chapter 7

# Moving from Sit to Write

## Wrapping up the Sit experiments

All of the experiments in the Sit section can help you prepare your mind for writing. Perhaps you have clarified your intentions. Perhaps you have confronted your internal gremlins. Perhaps you have cleared your mind of concerns to make room for writing to happen. Perhaps you have decided on the contexts and rewards that will lead to a writing habit. Perhaps you have experienced your own ability to cultivate sparks of inspiration and keep them burning. If you are not yet ready to tackle the actual work of writing, consider going back to some of the Sit experiments to help you get your mind and body ready. For a quick review, Table 1 contains the morals from the Sit experiments.

Table 1: Collected Morals from the Sit Experiments

| Sit# | Category | Moral |
|------|----------|-------|
| Sit 1 | Intentions | Reading develops the mind's eye. |
| Sit 2 | Intentions | A commonplace book can be a source of inspiration. |
| Sit 3 | Intentions | Extend what already works before worrying about problems. |
| Sit 4 | Intentions | Setting an intention can help you step away from doubts. |
| Sit 5 | Gremlins | Nobody was born writing well, but many learn with practice. |
| Sit 6 | Gremlins | Your voice may be just what someone needs to hear. |
| Sit 7 | Habits | Clear your brain for writing by putting away what went before. |
| Sit 8 | Habits | Simple steps change behavior. |
| Sit 9 | Habits | Use context and rewards to train your brain's habit system. |
| Sit 10 | Habits | Become aware of obstacles so you can move around them. |
| Sit 11 | Habits | Let avoiding one task motivate you to do another. |
| Sit 12 | Inspiration | Find your muse inside yourself. |
| Sit 13 | Inspiration | Constraints may be advantages in disguise. |

Now it is time to move on to the actual work of collecting ideas, putting words on the page, and revising them until they sing.

# Writing Experiments

The experiments in this part of the book revolve around getting the writing done. There are twenty-six Write experiments. To make them easier to navigate, I have organized them into three categories:

- **Imagine:** Writers play with ideas mentally, perhaps without writing anything down. They may decide what belongs, try out different structures, collect stories, and even look through old writing for pieces to repurpose.

- **Draft:** Writers get a first draft down on paper without worrying about quality. Everything produced in this stage can be changed later. But without the first draft, nothing happens.

- **Edit:** Grateful for the first draft, writers make the piece better and better. Done well, this also occurs in phases, moving from big picture to tiny detail.

———————//———————

Initially, I divided the Write experiments into two categories, Draft and Edit. I strongly believe these activities need to be done separately. Then I realized that I do a lot of the work of writing without a writing implement. I walk around thinking about ideas. I have conversations with myself about ideas while I wash dishes. I discuss ideas with friends. I called the third type of activity Imagine. To write, you need to imagine, draft, and edit.

## Take Stock

Thinking of writing as a multi-step activity is a professional approach to writing. Taking stock of your own strengths and preferences, you can make informed choices about how to handle the steps that come less naturally to you. You can choose to get better at them, perhaps using experiments in this book. If you have the means, you can choose to hire others to do them, for example by hiring a ghostwriter or editor. When outsourcing certain steps, you'll be better at supervising others if you clearly understand what needs to be done.

Table 2 is my personal summary of the steps involved in writing, at least for non-fiction, which is the kind of writing I encounter most often. Fiction writing might include other steps, such as character and plot development. Use this table to identify your strengths and areas needing more development. I recommend indicating for each step whether you find it easy, middling, or hard. Easy steps are the ones you already find fun and rewarding. Continue to enjoy them. Hard steps are your greatest challenges. Experiments in this section of the book may help you make them easier. Middling steps could be tackled later.

*Table 2: Steps in a Writing Process*

| Step Description | Stage |
|---|---|
| Imagining the intended audience, capture the big picture idea. | Imagine → Exit when you have enough ideas to start drafting |
| Decide on the overall form. Will it be a book, blog post, magazine article, podcast script, or other? | |
| Determine the concepts to be covered and the stories needed to illustrate them. | |
| Determine the structure. How should concepts be ordered so that they build on each other and so you don't rely on a concept before you have introduced it? | |
| Write the first draft. You may end up writing the first drafts of different components independently. | Draft → Exit when draft seems complete |
| Set what you've written aside at least overnight. Then write a second draft, based on the way it makes you feel now. | |
| Edit at the conceptual and structural levels. Pay attention to the ending and the beginning. Make sure you don't bury the lede, unless that creates effective dramatic tension. | Edit → Exit when ready to publish |
| Seek feedback at a more detailed level. How does the argument flow? Do the transitions work? In this step, take out paragraphs that no longer belong for whatever reason. | |
| Edit at the paragraph level. Do you start new paragraphs when you start new thoughts? Do paragraphs have topic sentences and transitions? Are you repeating yourself unnecessarily? | |
| Edit at the diction and punctuation level. This is another chance to look for redundancy. | |
| Read the piece out loud to catch errors and awkward spots. | |

The order in the table may imply that you finish all the imagining before you start drafting and likewise that you finish all the drafting before you start editing. Usually, people cycle through the activities multiple times before a piece is complete. While drafting, you may run out of ideas before the piece is complete, or you may feel more like editing on a particular day.

Try not to spend much time drafting ideas that do not belong in your book or editing paragraphs you later delete.

This table does not include entries for publishing because that topic is covered in the Share chapters. If you find you have a drawer or a computer folder full of pieces you have written but never shown to others, perhaps it is time to skip forward to Share. Sharing creates a feedback loop that contributes to skill growth. When you engage with others, you see what works and where your writing loses people. Having others engage with your work helps you learn how to hold their attention. Often that generates more ideas so that the process becomes easier with each iteration.

# Chapter 8

# Write Experiments: Imagine

*Hands, do what you're bid:*
*Bring the balloon of the mind*
*That bellies and drags in the wind*
*Into its narrow shed.*
 ~ William Butler Yeats, *The Balloon of the Mind*

Of all the things you could write, what do want to write? Where do you find the stories, concepts, and activities to support your theme? What kind of writing can you do while you are going for a walk or doing chores?

This is the time to playfully arrange and rearrange thoughts until the next step becomes clear.

# Write Experiment 1: Decide What Goes In

## STORY: CHOOSING WHAT TO SHARE

John Yeager had been a high school teacher, a sports coach, a university professor, and a business consultant over a long career. Feeling a passion to share what his years of experience had taught him, he decided to write a book. After a few months of writing, he was overwhelmed by the sheer magnitude of the job.

John created a list of the topics he had taught students, athletes, fellow coaches, and business clients. Looking at his list, I was reminded of the lines from W. B. Yeats on the previous page.

What could he do to bring this balloon of his mind into a narrow shed? I passed on to him the advice I had gotten from a coaching mentor about business development: "If you yell, 'Hey you!' to a busy crowd, nobody pays any attention. If you yell, 'Hey Ben!' all the Bens in the crowd will turn to look at you." It's important to figure out the audience you can best serve. It won't be everybody.

John figured that the first step was to pick a particular audience and a particular purpose for his book. Looking at all the roles he had played, he believed he could make the most difference writing for sports coaches about self-awareness and other-forms of awareness needed to be true leaders. Many coaches had said things to him like, "If it weren't for the athletes, I'd feel totally on top of my job," or "How can I get this year's team to show the same level of energy and passion that last year's team did?" or "I've got a roster of wannabe stars, but I want to have a team."

He thought he could help.

## OBSERVATIONS

Most people could fill many books with what they have learned, experienced, and created in their lives. Not only do they have many memories, opinions, and facts in their minds, but these elements are interconnected in ways that create extremely complex mental landscapes.

One of the hard lessons of writing is to realize that other people don't need our entire mental landscapes. Their minds are full of their own memories, opinions, and facts. What they may welcome from us are insights and information to help them organize their own mental states.

## STEPS

While you are writing a particular piece, do the following at least once. For books, it may be helpful to do it multiple times, either periodically or whenever you feel overwhelmed.

1.  Write a sketch of the audience you want to reach and the way you want to change them.

2.  Make a list of topics you want to cover in your book.

3.  For each topic on the list, ask yourself:

    •   Do the people in my audience need to know this?

    •   Will they be interested?

    •   Will this help me achieve my purpose with them?

    •   If I have already discussed this topic elsewhere, am I saying it from a sufficiently different point of view that it will add rather than dilute?

4.  Unless you can say a resounding "Yes" to all four questions, set the topic aside.

---

**MORAL** Your audience wants only a small fraction of everything you know.

# Write Experiment 2: Play with Ideas

## STORY: LETTING IDEAS BUBBLE UP

In 1987, Dr. John B. Smith, a professor at the University of North Carolina, helped our team of software engineers start writing the specifications for a brand-new networking protocol. It was very unusual for us to work on a *green field* project, that is, to get to start from scratch rather than make changes to an existing base. Our team leader hired John because she was worried that we might be stymied by the blank page. We followed John's directions carefully. As you read the steps below, imagine six software engineers sitting around a table doing absolutely nothing for 10 minutes, then scribbling madly on yellow stickies, and then gathering at the whiteboard to arrange the ideas. When we started writing after this exercise, we each knew exactly what to do.

I am intentionally putting the steps before the observations in this experiment because I think the observations make more sense once you understand the steps.

## STEPS

1.  Decide on a general writing topic. It could be the theme of your book, chapter, or blog.

2.  Gather supplies: a timer, a stack of yellow stickies, and a fat-tipped marker. You will also need a wall, whiteboard, or a large piece of butcher paper on which to mount the yellow stickies later.

3.  Set the timer for 10 minutes. Close your eyes and let your thoughts wander. Don't particularly try to think about the writing theme.

4.  When the timer dings, start writing ideas on yellow stickies, just one or two words per idea. Write big enough so you can read your words from a distance. Work fast. Don't dwell on any particular idea longer

than writing it down. The ideas can be concepts, stories, activities, special details, whatever bubbles up.

5. When your ideas slow down, attach the yellow stickies to your working surface. Spread them out so that you can read each yellow sticky. Step back to look at them all together.

6. Start moving the yellow stickies around to gather ideas into clumps. Put similar ideas together or put contrasting ideas together. Try out different approaches.

7. Transform the clumps into an outline that you can use to start working on your product. What is each clump's header? What are the parts?

8. In subsequent writing sessions, you can pick one yellow sticky to use as your writing prompt. Put it back on the board with a big checkmark when you finish the first draft.

9. Whenever you feel stuck, look at the whole picture again. Are there any stickies that need to be moved? Do other orders emerge? Do other ideas need to be captured? Your sticky pad is still there for new thoughts, and the stickies can be moved around to shape different connections. Repeat the whole process as needed.

### OBSERVATIONS

I have used this approach with several stuck writers. There are two aspects to it that can be used separately or together to make progress.

Somehow the period of quiet as the timer ticks down loosens up the stranglehold that the conscious mind puts on creative thinking. Writing down the ideas fast lets them flow.

The design firm, Ideo, has formulated seven rules of good brainstorming. There is a link to Ideo's brainstorming approach in this book's resources. This experiment directly invokes at least four of them: defer judgment; encourage wild ideas; be visual; go for quantity.

Rearranging the yellow stickies on the wall is one way to play physically and visually with the structure of your piece. Look for balance: Are there too many ideas in one clump and too few in another? You might want to introduce color as another visual clue, for example copying key concepts onto green stickies and story topics onto pink ones.

I've seen several people put entire books in order with multi-colored stickies on a wall. See an example in Figure 1, which shows writing ideas on colored stickies arranged on a wall. This can be done as a team or solo activity.

Figure 1: Brainstorming with Colored Stickies in Action

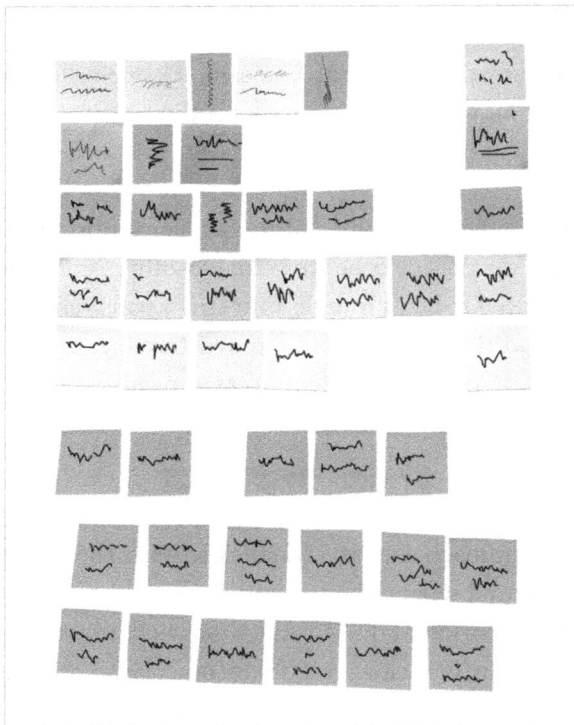

MORAL A playful spirit welcomes new ideas and new ways to arrange them.

# Write Experiment 3: Figure Out Manageable Chunks

## STORY: SORTING CONTENT

Even though Josie had a clear mental picture of the book she wanted to write for elementary teachers about enhancing creativity in the class-room, she had trouble getting anything written. She found herself sitting down to write and mentally hop-skipping over all the ideas she wanted to get across.

Working with a writing coach, Josie figured out that her book needed three forms of content: concepts, stories to illustrate them, and exercises to practice them. Once she decided these were the right units for her writing, she made a spreadsheet with all the concepts in one column, all the story ideas in another, and all the exercises in a third. She labeled stories and exercises with matching concepts. Whenever she had a new idea, she added it to her spreadsheet.

The spreadsheet became her writing to-do list. If she felt like writing a story, she picked one and got to work. If she felt ready to explain a con-cept, that's where she spent her time. Exercises were generally the easiest for her to create, so she did them in her less energetic writing sessions.

## OBSERVATIONS

Any big project needs to be broken down into manageable pieces so that it isn't overwhelming.

I once heard someone explain that it is inefficient to cover both strategy and tactics in the same business meeting because they involve different kinds of thinking. It takes people time to switch between big picture ideas and detailed execution. The speaker made the recommen-dation that leaders cover these topics in completely separate meetings.

Creating the list of concepts, stories, and exercises was big picture thinking, with Josie keeping the entire book in mind as she figured out what elements she needed to get the broad idea across. When she wrote a story, she could focus on the details needed to make it come alive without worrying about where the story fit in the overall picture.

Josie's units may be useful to you if you are working on a self-help or how-to book. If you are working on a memoir, you might choose periods of time. Sometimes it makes sense to separate a major activity into phases and use the phases as units.

—————— // ——————

When Marie-Josée Shaar and I wrote *Smarts and Stamina*, our writing accelerated dramatically when we decided to have 10 short chapters each for sleep, food, mood, and exercise. Once we created a structure for each unit, we flew through the writing. See more about unit structure in Write Experiment 12 in Chapter 9.

——— **STEPS** ———

1. Figure out the units that make the most sense for you. Does the concept-story-exercise approach work? If not, try reading books that you find easy to follow. What do their units seem to be? Would they work for you?

2. Once you've settled on a tentative structure, start your lists. Be aware that you don't have to finish your lists before you start writing. You can always revisit them to add or prune.

3. Consult your list whenever you need to figure out what to write next.

4. Optionally label the items in your list Easy or Hard. That way, whether you have a small or large window of time to write, you can quickly select something that fits.

5. Check off the items as you draft them.

———— // ————

It's very satisfying to see progress. I have a spreadsheet to check off the many pieces of this book. I also use it to make sure that I do not reuse names in multiple stories and that my stories have roughly as many male as female characters. I also use it to keep track of permissions that I need to gather. Figure 2 shows some of the columns of my spreadsheet for the rows that track the Sit Experiments.

### Figure 2: Tracking Spreadsheet

|        | Title | Chapter | Draft | Review | Gender | Name | Permission |
|--------|-------|---------|-------|--------|--------|------|------------|
|        | Sit Introduction | | | 15/3/2021 | M | Brian B. | Granted |
| Sit 1 | Read with Intention | Intentions | Y | 15/7/2021 | F | Jolie | |
| Sit 2 | Commonplace book | Intentions | Y | 20/10/2021 | F | Sally B. | Asked |
| Sit 3 | Recall Successes | Intentions | Y | 26/10/2020 | F | Jane | |
| Sit 4 | Set Intention | Intentions | Y | 26/10/2020 | M | Jamal | |
| Sit 5 | I'll never be a writer | Gremlins | Y | 12/11/2020 | M | Jerry | |
| Sit 6 | Who cares what I say | Gremlins | Y | 21/1/2021 | F | Jacinta | |
| Sit 7 | Reset Ritual | Habits | Y | 12/11/2020 | F | Janice | |
| Sit 8 | Build habits | Habits | Y | 29/3/2021 | F | Sharon D. | Granted |
| Sit 9 | Build Habits redux | Habits | Y | 1/11/2021 | M | Jeb | |
| Sit 10 | Use WOOP | Habits | Y | 4/2/2021 | M | Jared | |
| Sit 11 | Procrastination aikido | Habits | Y | 24/11/2020 | F | Me | |
| Sit 12 | Cultivate inspiration | Inspiration | Y | 12/4/2021 | F | Jasmine | |
| Sit 13 | Welcome constraints | Inspiration | Y | 24/11/2020 | M | Phil H. | |

**MORAL** Break a big project down into manageable steps.

# Write Experiment 4: Prime Intuition

## STORY: WRITING WITHOUT A PEN

I originally thought of this experiment as *Let Writing Go On In Your Head*. I do so much of my own writing work while I'm cleaning up the kitchen or weeding the garden. As ideas flow through my mind, I try them on for size and play with different ways to express them. Other people tell me they do similar mental exploration while they are walking the dog. I don't worry about capturing the ideas as they flow. I have faith that any really good ideas will stay close enough to the surface of my mind that I can reach them when I'm back at my keyboard.

## OBSERVATIONS

This experiment is an intentional way to broaden access to the creativity of the unconscious mind. There is so much more stored in our minds than the thoughts that bubble around on the conscious surface. There is a data bank of experiences and observations that go back as far as memory stretches. We absorbed some without even being aware of doing so. Under the surface, intuition searches and connects them in novel ways all the time. Many people have experienced having an idea pop to the conscious surface fully formed, often when doing something relatively relaxing such as taking a shower.

The technique in this experiment comes from Nil Demircubuk, a consultant who teaches clients to use intuition and intellect in tandem. First, she helps them listen to their intuitions. Then she reminds them to evaluate what emerges. Not all intuitions are right or even useful. Using intuition and intellect together augments creativity.

The critical ingredient is what Nil calls priming for intuition. She bases it partly on research by Dr. Kenneth Gilhooly about creative problem-solving. He found that people who loaded the problem into their minds and then immediately did something else for a short period tended to be more productive creatively than people who immediately jumped into problem-solving. He called this the immediate incubation period.

Nil's approach alternates incubation periods that open the mind to the subconscious with direct work periods where the ideas are used in conscious problem-solving.

## STEPS

1. Load your mind with the task you want to accomplish in your writing. Do you want to tell a story, explain a concept, or capture a scene? Remember the goal in detail, and review any obstacles. You are loading a problem to be solved into your subconscious.

2. Set the task aside. To prime for intuition, go do something else, preferably something that relaxes you and lifts your mood. Go for a walk, play a video game, listen to pleasant music. The important point is that you incubate before you start the conscious work.

3. Work on the task consciously. Have a good go at putting the idea into words.

4. When you feel stuck, return to step 2 for further incubation. Alternate between steps 2 and 3 until you are out of time for this writing session.

5. If you haven't finished the piece by the end of this session, use the same sequence in the next session. Start by loading the task into your mind, then alternate between incubating and working.

## POSSIBLE ADDITION

Nil has combined this approach with the Pomodoro™ Technique to create what she calls the Menemen Technique. Pomodoro is Italian for tomato, and Menemen is a Turkish breakfast dish of scrambled eggs with tomatoes. Nil figures that eggs represent incubation.

The Pomodoro Technique involves alternating 25-minute work periods with 5-minute play periods. The originator of the technique, Francesco Cirillo, named the approach after his tomato-shaped timer, as shown in Figure 3.

*Figure 3: A Pomodoro Timer*
*(iStock.com/AllesandroZocc)*

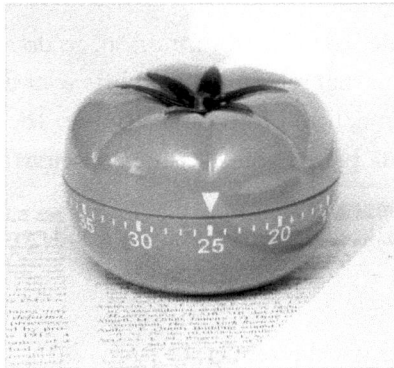

The Menemen Technique alternates work and play, but starts with play once the problem has been loaded into the brain.

Looking at the steps above, just add setting the timer as you move from step to step: 5 minutes for the incubation periods, 25 minutes for the work periods.

---

**MORAL**  Reach into your life-long well of experiences for inspiration.

# Write Experiment 5: Collect Story Seeds

## STORY: THREE TYPES OF STORIES

One of my favorite psychologists, Albert Bandura, once said that psychologists are terrible at the social diffusion of ideas. They do their research, learn interesting things about humans, and yet collectively have little influence on human behavior. Toward the end of his career, he decided to put his energies into creating serial dramas to address behavior changes needed in particular places. His topics included enrollment in adult literacy programs in Mexico, delaying age of marriage for girls in India, and safe sex practices to reduce the prevalence of AIDS in sub-Saharan Africa. He worked with local governments and local media experts to produce long-running soap operas that addressed the chosen topics.

According to Dr. Bandura, a serial drama needs three types of substories to change behavior:

1.  Stories showing the desired behavior and how it affects people

2.  Stories of the undesired behavior

3.  Stories of people in transition from the undesired behavior to the desired behavior.

Around the world, people gathered to watch or listen to these stories the same way many of us watched Downton Abbey. One article about the Mexican series indicated that enrollment in adult literacy programs increased by a factor of nine among serial drama viewers. There are links to articles about Bandura's serial dramas in the book's resources.

## OBSERVATIONS

Stories are sticky. We are much more likely to remember them than the concepts they illustrate. They also help us see how particular concepts change shape when they are applied in particular contexts. Stories of good behavior give us everyday heroes to emulate. Stories of bad behavior help us see consequences to avoid. Stories of transitions help us believe that change is possible.

We live lives of constant story. We have an exchange in the grocery store that annoys or delights us. We experience a kindness or a meanness. We get an email that perplexes us. Having an alertness for the stories as they arise is like gathering seeds to plant next year. They may be dormant until a need arises to write a story about a particular point. If we collect story seeds as we go along, we're more likely to write stories that move others.

My husband used to have phone calls with his mother every other day. He kept a note card in his pocket to jot down things that might interest her as they happened. Lively and engaging conversations occurred between them because he collected story seeds for her.

## STEPS

1.  Believe that your life is full of stories that may be useful to your writing.

2.  Keep a note card or a phone app like Evernote to jot down words to remind you of things you observe that might make good stories. Using the story seed metaphor, these would need to be planted, watered, and put in the light to sprout. They need never be shared with others in this form.

3. For a particular writing project, consult your list of story seeds. Pick ones that fit. Make a list so that you can write them in even small fragments of time.

4. When you finish writing a piece, especially if you are calling for behavior change, check the balance of good behavior, bad behavior, and transition stories. That's not to say that every piece needs an equal number of all three. But the balance is worth considering.

---

**MORAL**   Collect stories as you see them occur.

# Write Experiment 6: Mine Stories for Concepts

## STORY: FINDING CONCEPTS IN STORIES

Joellen was very good at leading workshops on becoming more resilient at work. She had an extensive collection of funny, touching, and believable stories that helped people grasp and remember her messages. The previous experiment was about collecting story seeds. Joellen was a masterful collector. As she taught and went about her life, she was always alert to new challenges, always looking for the people who came through better than others, and always curious about what made the difference.

When Joellen took stock getting ready to write a book, she realized that she was strong on stories and weak on concepts. She knew how to show rather than tell to a fault. Now she needed to insert concepts so that people could grasp more than one story at a time.

To get unstuck, Joellen wrote down a list of all her stories. She looked at the list for common themes. At first, not much came up. Then she decided to express the key takeaway for each story in three to five words. Here are some examples that she discovered: *Importance of friends. Resilience can be built. First calm down. Take inventory of assets.*

When she finished, she had a list of concepts that she could start shaping into the skeleton of her book. She pictured some as part of the spine that held other ideas up, some as limbs that moved the structure forward, and some as the digits that served as finishing touches.

## OBSERVATIONS

Stories are really important. They make ideas come alive in people's minds. Once that happens, ideas are more likely to stick.

But concepts are also important. They capture ideas in general terms, unmuddied by personality quirks. They are ready for application in completely different contexts. In the complex moments of their lives, people find it easier to sort through concepts for guidance than to recall stories looking for ones that address similar circumstances. Once a concept is found, it might serve as the keyword to bring relevant stories back to mind.

## STEPS

1. Write down a list of your stories. Assign them numbers or other identifiers.

2. Get a yellow sticky pad and a marking pen.

3. Go through your stories. For each, figure out the key takeaway (or takeaways). Figure out how to say it in three to five words.

4. If you've already identified a particular takeaway for a different story in your list, add the story identifier to the yellow sticky created earlier for the other story.

5. If you haven't seen this takeaway associated with any other stories, write it on a new yellow sticky along with the story identifier.

6. When you are finished, create a list of key concepts cross-referenced to stories. This might be a spreadsheet or an arrangement of yellow stickies on a whiteboard.

7. Use a white board or wall to play around with arranging the takeaways into clumps that belong together. This might give you a head start on the structure of your piece.

---

**MORAL** Concepts may be easier to carry around in the brain than stories.

# Write Experiment 7: Repurpose Old Writing

## STORY: LOOKING IN A DESK DRAWER

Judith was an active member of a writing group. She tried hard to submit her pieces on time. One day, she drew a complete blank. Nothing came to mind to write about. She turned away from trying to write to clean out her desk drawers. As she sorted through old papers deciding whether to shred, recycle, or keep, she came across a paper she had written 10 years earlier as an honors project. She sat right down to read it.

"Hmm, this is good stuff. I had some good ideas back then. But nobody will ever read my senior honors paper. Even my mother didn't read it. Maybe I could take these ideas to create something new. After all, I don't completely agree with myself of 10 years ago, but I still think I had some important things to say."

That was the start of an article that Judith published several places online. Her initial paper had been full of quotations from other people. As she updated it, she kept asking herself, "What do I believe now?" The resulting paper was in Judith's voice with Judith's ideas in place of most of the references to authorities. Ten years of further experience made her much more confident about her own ideas. She also made the piece more vivid by adding stories that came from her personal experiences and the experiences of the people around her.

## OBSERVATIONS

It is perfectly legitimate to update, repurpose, and extend something written before. One of my closest friends told me the main lesson she learned while working on her doctorate was to get the most mileage out of whatever she wrote.

Academic researchers might need to protect against their repurposed work being seen as self-plagiarizing, since the academic world is very concerned about publication numbers as a measure of accomplishment. They can always reframe their ideas and cite their previous work to make it clear that there is something new. Or they can publish it in a different format for a different audience, perhaps cutting down technical terms to make the piece more accessible.

For the rest of us, reusing ideas, particularly when we extend them with new stories, can be a significant contribution to our writing efforts. At the very least, we show that new experiences have reinforced rather than shaken what we believed before. Or perhaps we have been changed by experience and updated our points of view. That can also be informative.

## STEPS

1.  If you are feeling stuck with writing, look through writing you've done before. Here are some possible sources:

    *   High school, college, and graduate school papers. Perhaps the oldest ones are not directly reusable, but they may remind you of questions that you've been considering for a long time. I have a notebook of high school papers and a box full of college papers. My graduate school papers are on a CD. School papers have a very small audience, usually you and the teacher. Does the idea merit wider exposure?

    *   Annual holiday letters. These might suggest story seeds. For more on story seeds, see Write Experiment 5 in Chapter 8.

    *   Articles you started but never finished.

    *   Old email arguments with a friend or colleague. I recently had an email argument with an old mentor about how a new profession starts licensing and policing its members. That might be the seed of a blog post, with two points of view that conflict in certain areas and coincide in others.

2. Old pictures that suggest stories. For example, I have a picture of my grandfather and his four brothers in their different military uniforms from World War I. There might be a story there.

3. If you've selected an opinion piece, decide whether to frame your new piece as agreeing or arguing with your former self. Either way works and can be interesting. Do you want to show yourself changing over time or remaining constant to a particular value? Have some fun arguing or agreeing with yourself.

4. Consider your audience. What do they know and want to learn? Often this means removing jargon and reworking the language of academia to make the ideas more accessible to the general public.

5. Consider the needs of two groups: your audience, and the researchers whose work you cited in the original. In my opinion, your greater responsibility is to your readers. You can always give credit to someone whose work shaped your thinking in an end note. In-text citations and precise descriptions of various research programs are likely to distract or bore a lay audience.

6. If you are citing research, check to see whether the results you found interesting before still hold up today. One study does not constitute proof. Has the research been replicated? Does the result hold up in meta-analyses? Has it been superseded by subsequent work?

---

**MORAL** New writing can emerge from old documents and pictures.

# Chapter 9

# Write Experiments: Draft

*"Now practically even better news than that of short assignments is the idea of shitty first drafts. All good writers write them. This is how they end up with good second drafts and terrific third drafts."*
~ Anne Lamott, *Bird by Bird*

If you find writing the first draft the most difficult part of writing, put Anne Lamott's words where you can see them often. A first draft doesn't have to be long, and it doesn't have to be perfect. It just needs to be created.

# Write Experiment 8: Draft Without Editing

## STORY: STAYING AWAY FROM THE DELETE KEY

When I was in college, I typed my papers on a manual typewriter. I also made some money by typing other people's papers. When I typed the wrong character, I had to roll the paper up, erase or white out the mistake, and then roll the paper back very carefully, hoping it hadn't gotten out of alignment.

As a result, I have always loved writing on a computer. It's so flexible. I can write, rearrange, leave gaps, and come back later to make changes. No more white-out. I'm not committed to what comes from my fingers initially.

However, to become productive, I had to learn to keep my finger off the delete key when writing first drafts. In the early days, I might write a sentence, think, "That's not right," and erase it. Sometimes when a session ended, it seemed that I had written 1000 words and erased 990 of them.

What really helps me is to think of two writers in my brain. Drafter gets to write whatever she wants. The order doesn't matter. The word choice doesn't matter. The quality of the ending and beginning doesn't matter. Her job is to get the basic ideas on the page. Then Editor takes over. Editor may sniff at what Drafter left her to work with, but actually she's relieved to be able to do what she does best: pick effective words, make sure sentences can be parsed by other people, make sure the sequence makes sense, and so on. Drafter captures the big picture. Editor makes the writing flow.

## OBSERVATIONS

Drafting and editing are very different activities. They draw on different mental faculties. Drafting is a big picture, imaginative activity, making something out of nothing. Editing is careful, particular work. Drafting requires turning judgment off or at least down. Editing needs judgment to be turned up high. The question for drafting is, "Have I captured the idea?" The questions for editing vary. They include, "Will other people be able to understand it?" and "Do I like the way it sounds?"

Drafter and Editor don't do well working at the same time. One has a heavy foot on the accelerator, while the other is pressing on the brake. When they are both active at the same time, a writer spends a great deal of energy without moving very far forward.

**STEPS**

1. As you start writing, decide whether you are going to be drafting a new piece or editing an existing piece. You can do both in the same session. For example, you could spend the first half of the session drafting and the second half editing what you drafted. Just avoid doing them simultaneously. Mentally note when you flip into the other activity.

2. If you are drafting, push any judgmental voices in your head aside. Tell your editor it will have its turn. Mentally put a cover over the Delete key.

3. If you are editing, start with mental gratitude to your drafting self for giving you something to form and polish.

**MORAL** Use either the accelerator or the brake, not both at the same time.

# Write Experiment 9: Just Do It

Jabir was a member of a writing group that met weekly. He missed two sessions when he could have submitted writing for review. He finally confessed that he was so badly blocked that nothing was coming out. We brainstormed ways he could get past his blockage. All group members mentioned times when they found writing just too hard. Jabir found it encouraging to see that he was not alone and that others were not disgusted with him for failing to meet his deadlines. They all found writing difficult. Most of the suggestions ended up being some form of "Just do it." Just write three sentences. Just write for five minutes. Just write whatever comes to mind.

Jabir admitted that he was afraid of other people judging him harshly for his writing. The group helped him see the value of vulnerability. Opening himself up added power to the words he was writing. They were interested in what he revealed. Jabir went from being paralyzed by fear to acknowledging the fear and moving past it.

## OBSERVATIONS

Acceptance and Commitment Therapy revolves around the idea that people heal by accepting what cannot be changed and committing themselves to change what can be changed. That doesn't mean it is simple.

Let us assume that the fear of writing is something that can be changed if you have the will to do so. The ideas below may help you just do it.

**STEPS**

1.  These suggestions are gifts offered to you by other writers. Read through them and select any that resonate with you.

    *   Breon Michel says, "What's helped me the most has more to do with learning how to work with fear and less to do with specific writing tactics. It takes a lot of courage to be authentic, but in doing this inner work, I've noticed a direct effect on my writing. I have found it helpful to focus on caring less about how to say something so it will appease others and more about speaking from my heart, regardless of how it's received."

    *   Natalie Griffin says, "I make a deal with myself that I'll just write for ten minutes. Ten minutes only, that's not so long, right? Once I start writing, initially it's hard, but after ten minutes have passed, the largest challenge of just getting started has been beaten, and I find that I have the strength/inspiration to continue. What I produce might not be great when I'm feeling blocked and uninspired, but it's a place to jump off from, and then I have something to show for my efforts at the end of the day."

    *   Manu Chatterjee says, "When I get stuck, I force myself to write two sentences. Sometimes funny things happen." Author's note: there is a link to the Medium article Manu wrote on this subject in this book's resources.

2.  Many people recommend writing morning pages, an idea from Julia Cameron's *The Artist's Way*. For morning pages, sit down every morning and write three pages longhand without editing. Anything goes, no matter how mundane or weird. It is a way to practice getting past the internal censor that keeps us from being creative.

---

**MORAL** Find a way to turn attention from the fear of writing to the work.

# Write Experiment 10:
# Write about Not Being Able to Write

Jacob was writing a combination memoir and how-to book about deal-ing with a child with a gambling addiction. Things were humming along until one day, he found himself blocked. He'd sit down to write, and no words would come out.

After several days of feeling blocked, he decided to write about not being able to write. He described what it felt like in his body. He recorded the thoughts that were spinning through his head just as he heard them. He wrote about where he was in his narrative. As he did so, he realized that he had reached perhaps the crux of his story. He didn't even want to think about the event that came next in his narrative. By writing about his resistance, he was able to move around the difficult subject indirectly at first. That indirectness helped him see clearly what he needed to do next. He was now ready to write the difficult story. Once he had it captured, things started to hum along again.

Jennifer Cory, one of my writing friends, wrote, "Regarding writ-er's block, a dear friend and professional writer once shared this advice: 'Write the log jam.' We all have things that need to be voiced before we can get to the stuff we want to be sharing with the world. To free up the mind sometimes we must first write about those things we never wanted to write about and get them out of the way."

## OBSERVATIONS

I have seen this experiment work several times, and it always seems like magic. How does focusing on the actual experience of being blocked help us get unblocked? I speculate that it works in the same paradox-ical way that noticing wandering thoughts works in meditation. Some meditation teachers say to name the thoughts because that loosens their hold. By writing about the experience, we take down the barriers of self-judgment. When we write about exactly what we are experiencing in the blocked moments, we are practicing with the most accessible content at that moment.

Sometimes the words written about being blocked get put aside. Sometimes the words turn into a story that may be an important element of a larger product. At the very least, you're practicing the art of writing, of capturing emotions and thoughts in words.

## STEPS

1. To get in the right mood for looking inside and not fighting what you find, read *The Guest House*, a poem by 13th century Persian poet, Jalāl al-Dīn Rumi. There is a link to a translation by Coleman Barks in this book's resources.

2. Put your feelings about writing into words. The following questions may help:

   - What does this reluctance to write feel like in my body?

   - When have I felt this way before? How have I gotten past blocks in other domains?

   - If there is a thought on the doorstep that I am afraid to let in, what is it? What does the fear feel like?

3. Consider what you might tell a friend or colleague experiencing a similar block.

4. When you finish thoroughly describing your experience of being blocked, save your writing in a place you can find the next time you feel blocked. You might be able to take up the story again when that happens, or you might find it interesting to see how your feelings of being blocked have changed.

5. Optionally share your piece with a friend or mentor who might help you see even further.

6. Consider whether there is a story in your writing that might be useful to you in some public context.

---

**MORAL** Even being blocked can be a launchpad for writing.

# Write Experiment 11:
# Write Daily and Keep Records

## STORY: A LITTLE GOES A LONG WAY

Janet is a post-doc in nursing. In addition to conducting new research, her job right now is to get papers published. Some are offshoots of her dissertation. Some are growing out of side projects that she couldn't resist. Some are emerging from the interviews and data collection of her current study. A postdoc is a funny interval between doctoral work and an academic job. It gives people time to get a good start on publishing so that they don't perish when they start the hard work of teaching classes.

I keep my ears open for things that might help her manage her overfull days. Her toddler keeps her on the run. I was very excited to see an article from Stanford University titled *Writing Scholarly Manuscripts— Briskly and Well*. Just the ticket. When I reviewed it, I concluded the advice was general and simple enough to work for all writers.

## OBSERVATIONS

This experiment is based on two simple suggestions made by Richard Reis, the author of the Stanford article: Write daily for at least 15 to 30 minutes. Record minutes spent writing. My guess is that writing every day means you spend less time loading your brain before the writing can begin.

The Stanford article tested these simple writing practices with more than 90 faculty and graduate students. Ninety-five percent of the participants agreed that they got more done at a higher quality. Writing every day for as little as 30 minutes, participants found their annual rate of finishing manuscripts went up by a factor of at least two. Some experienced a six-fold increase. The Stanford article also suggests sharing writing records with a peer or coach. There is more about external accountability in the Share Experiments in Chapter 13.

=== **STEPS** ===

1. Decide on a minimum amount of time that you are going to spend writing every day. Perhaps start with 15 minutes and later increase it to 30 minutes.

2. Pick a time of day that you can commit to writing. For some, that's first thing in the morning, even before checking email. I've known people who get up 30 minutes earlier for their regular writing time. Other possibilities include right after lunch or in the evening after supper but before starting the relax-for-bed routine.

3. When you start writing, remember you're not responsible for completing the whole manuscript in this session, just moving the ball forward. You will write again tomorrow.

4. End the session by figuring out what you will write during the next session because it speeds up getting started each day. See more about doing this in Write Experiment 16, the last experiment in this chapter.

5. Keep track of the time you spend. That could be as simple as sending a coach or accountability partner a note with the number of minutes in the subject line, nothing inside the email unless you need to make an excuse for zero minutes. As you try to write even when you are tired, a little sick, or really busy, it helps to know that someone else is watching and can either challenge or applaud what you're doing.

6. Optionally, once you have an outline of what you want to achieve, start checking off the parts completed. I have a spreadsheet in which I put a date when an item is drafted. I also keep track of the date when each component is reviewed by somebody else. A section of this spreadsheet appears in Figure 2 in Chapter 8. The presence of filled-in columns is very encouraging.

**MORAL**  A little bit of writing every day can get a lot done.

# Write Experiment 12:
# Work Out Structure of Repeating Units

### STORY: PARTNERSHIP WITH MJ

When Marie-Josée Shaar (MJ) worked with people wanting to lose weight and/or become more fit, she found that many had no confidence in their ability to change for the better. There were just too many diet and exercise failures in their pasts.

MJ had studied the intricate connections among sleep, food, mood, and exercise. Making a change in one affects the other three. Thus, getting enough sleep tends to make it easier to resist food temptations. Feeling upbeat makes it easier to exercise. Her big idea was to suggest that people start with an area in which they had not had multiple failures in the past. For example, a client with a history of many failed diets may find that getting enough sleep makes it easier to eat smaller portions and exercise vigorously.

When I started working with MJ, she was bubbling with ideas to help people with sleep, food, mood, and exercise goals. Together we came up with the 50 activities that are described in our book, *Smarts and Stamina*. There are 10 activities each for sleep, food, mood, and exercise plus 10 activities to set oneself up for success. Now you see the first structure decision: to have 50 short chapters plus introductory materials for each of the five parts. Our writing really took off when we settled on a repeatable structure for each activity, as shown in Insert 7. The bolded headers are headers found in the book. The italicized header was different for each activity.

*Insert 7: Example of a Repeatable Structure*

*Catchy Title*

**Science Says:** 2 or 3 bullet points about research findings in everyday language

**Story:** Sketch of someone trying out the idea

**Build the Skills**

**Mindfulness:** Observing self before changing anything. Often getting a baseline.

**Plan and Execute:** The actual activity, which is generally actions and questions.

**Onward and Upward:** Reflecting on what worked well about the idea and how it could be incorporated in daily habits.

## OBSERVATIONS

Having the structure was immensely helpful, leading to an even-handed treatment of all 50 activities. We never felt stuck because there was always an outline with holes still to be filled in. When we had time to write, we could pick an unfinished activity and fill it out further. If one of us didn't feel like writing a story, we could leave it for the other to complete.

While not appropriate for every book, a repeatable structure can make a book easier to write. As described in Sit Experiment 13 in Chapter 6, constraints often lead to greater creativity, perhaps because they lead to focus. A repeated structure makes writing the whole book less daunting to the authors and makes reading it easier for the audience. It also makes it easier for readers to navigate back to a specific idea that resonated the first time through the book.

The repeatable structure could just be a section at the end of each chapter, such as *The Whirlwind Review* at the end of each major section of Chip and Dan Heath's book, *The Power of Moments*. Each whirlwind review lists the 8 to 10 key ideas that they want people to take from that section. The authors had to follow the discipline to identify and list the key ideas.

## STEPS

1. Look first at how you divide your work into units. Do you want to have 10 to 12 longer chapters or a large number of short chapters? Can the chapters be organized into parts, such that each part has one overall theme? For example, John Yeager's book, *The Coaching Zone*, contains 12 chapters organized according to three themes: effectively managing self, individual athletes, and entire teams.

2. Look through the books on your shelf to identify the repeatable structures they use. Are the chapters constructed the same way? Are there periodic summaries? Do you see repeated headers? Does each chapter start or end in a particular way? As a reader, which structures did you find most helpful?

3. Based on your awareness of the ways other people structured books, come up with a first draft of your own structure. It could be as simple as listing your chapter titles and then always starting a chapter with a statement describing its intended purpose. It might involve deciding how many stories you plan to tell and where to place them. Do you start with a story, follow it with an explanation, and then get into more detail? It might be using the same headers in each chapter. It might mean ending with an exercise or a summary.

4. Try it out for two or three units. Does it liberate you to get the job done, or do you feel constrained to write things that do not seem useful?

5.  Share the pieces written in your proposed structure with one or more friends, writing partners, or mentors. Do they find the structure helpful or obtrusive?

6.  Based on answers to questions in steps 4 and 5, make adjustments to the structure, and then proceed to use it in your writing.

7.  Whenever the structure feels unnatural or too formal, consider making adjustments.

———————//———————

*Sit Write Share* uses a repeated structure in the experiments. One beta reviewer, Andrew Soren, commented, "I really do love the structure - story —> evidence —> tactics —> moral. At first I wondered if the repetition would drive me crazy, but I quickly fell in love with its predictability."

**MORAL**  A well-chosen structure makes both writing and reading easier.

# Write Experiment 13: Capture Fleeting Moments

## STORY: CHERRIES ON THE WESTERN FRONT

My grandfather was an artillery officer on the Western Front in France in 1918. I suspect that his life conformed to the line published in the New York Times in 1915: "Months of boredom punctuated by moments of terror." Fortunately for me, he alleviated his boredom by writing home to his wife. She left the collection to me. I have his description of the day that news of the armistice traveled along the line. I also have his description of an afternoon on leave when he rode his horse along a country road looking for a place to get his first bath in two weeks. Along the way, he noticed some cherry trees full of fruit. Being alone and therefore not needing to be careful of his dignity, he stopped to climb a tree to eat his fill. Later he found a pond where he could wash. He ate cherries again on his way back to camp. This picture of an ordinary Oklahoma farmer in France would have disappeared at his death without his letters.

Many people have observed that history does little to record the lives of ordinary people living through the extraordinary events that make it into the history books. Writing in 2020, 2021, and beyond, we are making history collectively as we endure the COVID-19 pandemic and address the calls for social justice encapsulated in the Black Lives Matter movement. What we experience individually adds up to our collective history.

Even within our own lives, capturing specific moments can help. My sister had major surgery. As I helped care for her, I kept notes. What did the doctors say? What was she able to eat? What drains and tubes were taken out when? What walks was she able to take? On about day 40 of her recovery, she was feeling very, very low-spirited, "I'm never going to feel myself again." One of her friends sent her the notes we had posted on day 20, halfway to where she was then, to remind her how much she had advanced. If we had not created the records as we went along, she would have lacked comparison points. Downward comparison from the present to the past can be very helpful in difficult times.

## OBSERVATIONS

Imagine jumping forward 20 years. What you remember will be different from what you're actually experiencing right now. Memories are selective and change over time. What we remember most are the peak moments and the final moments of a particular event. The lower intensity middle moments tend to fade.

As we face the pandemic, I know that my ancestors made it through the 1918-1919 flu because I'm here. But what did they do? How did they manage the infection? How did they care for the people who were ill? What did they learn that might be useful to us? Can we collect information like that for our descendants?

## STEPS

1.  Set aside a few minutes to take notes about what's happening in your life. Here are some questions that might stimulate your thinking.

    •  What's hard about what's happening today?

    •  What have we figured out?

    •  Where have I advanced?

    •  What is working better for me than it did when I started along this path?

2.  Perhaps you are thinking, "Ugh, I am so busy. I can barely breathe. How could I possibly write things down?" Don't worry about grammar or spelling or proper diction or fluency. Just write. If that's still too hard, start the camera app on your phone and tell yourself the story. Or call a friend and record the conversation.

3.  Capture the events of right now with other people. Perhaps you could put the phone down in the middle of the table to record your dinner

conversation. Here are some questions that might make sense during a crisis like the pandemic. Some may also work in ordinary times.

- How do we divide up the chores? Who's doing what?

- How have we gotten the children and the rest of family involved in working out the solutions to our daily problems? What part of the responsibility are they picking up?

- Who are we reaching out to? Why did we choose those particular people?

- What makes us laugh?

- What aspects of the old life do we miss the most? How are we compensating?

- What is new that we actually like and want to continue?

- What is it that we want to remember about this particular day?

4. Send an email around to people in some group asking them to write a few sentences about a topic of mutual interest.

———————— // ————————

I did step 4 recently, sending my cousins and siblings an email on my grandfather's birthday with some quick memories of him. Seven people responded and then commented on each other's responses. It felt lovely to bring him to mind. Of course, we all remembered different things about him.

**MORAL** Writing about daily routines is capturing history in the making.

# Write Experiment 14: Try Speech-to-Text

## STORY: WRITING OUT LOUD

Jaclyn had a clear idea of the book she wanted to write, but she wasn't getting it done. She finally admitted to me that she was really good at writing once she had a first draft, but a blank piece of paper made her mind go blank.

I asked, "Could you explain your ideas to a friend?"

"Sure. That would be easy."

"What if you imagined a friend in front of you and explained your ideas into a speech-to-text program?"

"It's worth a try."

It was more than worth a try. Jaclyn wrote the first draft of most of her book in imaginary speeches to her good friends. She found an online transcription service that she could invoke from her smart phone. She'd go for walks, flip on the program, and start talking. Once she got the files back, she was off to the races.

She decided to include points of view from several experts in her field. She invited each to have coffee with her, put the phone in the middle of the table with the transcription program running, and started asking questions. For remote experts, she recorded Zoom conversations. She got some wonderful raw material, including moments of sparkling eloquence to quote in her book. She could also interact more dynamically because she wasn't trying to take notes.

## OBSERVATIONS

Jaclyn's first step toward a solution was recognizing what she found hard and what she found easy. The problem was half solved when she admitted to herself that she was fine once she had a first draft. That freed her to think of other ways to get a first draft rather than continuing to stare at a blank piece of paper in frustration.

When she tried transcription, Jaclyn found that she really enjoyed explaining concepts and telling stories out loud. Research in positive psychology indicates that people gain more when they build on their strengths than when they invest comparable effort in their weaknesses. Jaclyn knew that she really liked to talk, and she decided it wasn't worth her time to overcome her resistance to blank paper.

## STEPS

1.  Decide on the transcription approach you can afford and that will be good enough for your purposes. It does not have to be perfect.

2.  Google Docs and Word Online include dictation features that might be good enough. There are several online transcription services with different prices and quality levels that are particularly good for interviews. Services seem to be getting better and cheaper.

3.  Particularly if you are paying by the minute, prepare notes about what you want to accomplish during your speech-writing session. This will save you from wasting minutes fumbling around.

4.  Launch the program and start talking. Don't worry about repeating yourself or searching for the right word. You can always edit out the inevitable fluff later.

5.  Read through the transcript soon after you receive it in order to make corrections while the topic is still top of mind. No transcription service is perfect.

---

**MORAL** Talking can become writing.

# Write Experiment 15: Recover in a Hurry

This is an experiment I hope you never need to use, but chances are that it will someday be useful.

## STORY: DON'T PANIC

Jack spent a morning writing an article to be published online to support a podcast he was doing in a few days. It had been hard work. He had narrowed the topic, figured out good stories, organized points in a logical order, and written both a strong opening paragraph and a strong closure. Just before he was ready to declare himself done, his computer crashed. When he turned it back on, his file was nowhere. He figured he must have turned autosave off.

After frantically looking everywhere for it, he emailed me that he was not going to be able to submit anything to our writers' workshop. His words were just gone, and he was totally discouraged.

What I wrote back is captured in Insert 8.

*Insert 8: Advice on Loss of a File*

> This has happened to me more than once in my computer life. I will make one quick suggestion:
>
> The idea is in your head. If you open a document and just write what comes to mind WITHOUT WORRYING about the lost document, you will probably retrieve most of what you wrote. Often when this happens to me, the resulting document seems better than the original.

## OBSERVATIONS

Over the years, this has happened to me multiple times. I panic. I picture myself having to redo hours of work. But while doing the original writing, I made many small decisions that do not need to be made over again. What comes up if I just start over and type seems to be the essence of the piece without having to work my way through all the false starts and digressions that were part of the original writing. That's why, even though one document was now lost so I could do no direct comparisons, I often felt that the result of the quick rewrite was better than what I lost.

I am not alone in believing this. John Cleese of Monty Python fame tells a story about losing a script, rewriting it from memory, and then later finding the original. When he compared the two, the rewritten script was noticeably better.

## STORY CONTINUED:

Jack took a walk, then a shower, and then sat down at his keyboard. He wrote five pages in a little more than an hour. When we reviewed his document, it was clear that a lot more than an hour's worth of thought went into it.

## STEPS

1. If you lose a document, curb your tendency to panic.

2. Do something to relax. Take a walk, talk to a friend, or have a snack.

3. Open up a new file. Start typing what you remember of the contents of your lost document. Know that much of what you wrote is still in your head.

4. Make sure your autosave and file backup mechanisms are on and working properly. There is no point doing this any more than absolutely necessary.

**MORAL**  A lost document may still be in your head.

# Write Experiment 16:
# End a Session by Planning the Next Session

## STORY: WHAT SHOULD I WRITE TODAY?

When Jorge sits down to write, he often wonders, "What should I write today?" What he hears in his head may be a complete blank. By the time he has figured out what he needs to write, most of his available time is gone.

As he runs out of time, he hears his inner voice saying, "I'm just not a writer. Otherwise, I'd know what to write when I get a chance."

## OBSERVATIONS

Here's another way to think of it. When Jorge sits down to write, he is essentially starting cold. Having to think up what to write is one of the more difficult parts of writing. Athletes don't start practicing their most difficult skills without warming up with some easier moves. Why should writers?

## STEPS

1. At the end of a session when you are fully warmed up, don't stop before you have picked at least one idea to use as a jumping off point for your next writing session. It could be a concept you want to explain. It could be a story you want to tell. It could be a piece of writing that you want to edit. Make a note of your idea in a place that you will see the next time you sit down to write.

2. If nothing comes immediately to mind, consult your white board of stickies, story seed collection, or partially finished items.

3. It doesn't have to be just one idea. Perhaps you don't know whether you'll be in the mood to tell a story or explain a concept. You could pick one story idea and one concept. Picking between two possibilities is much easier than finding an idea from scratch.

4. Maybe you won't feel like writing anything new. It might be a good time to edit, polishing a rough draft.

5. Next time you sit down to write, warm up by writing a draft of the idea that you left yourself from the session before. If you have multiple ideas teed up, check your mood and do something that fits the moment.

### STORY CONTINUED:

Jorge is writing a book about baking bread. Today before finishing, he tees up his next concept to explain in tomorrow's writing session. He wants to explain why you need to resist the temptation to cut into the loaf when it first comes out of the oven because it hasn't finished baking. In case he feels like writing a story, he jots down a reminder of his daughter's response to the last cinnamon raisin loaf he baked.

MORAL Plan today for warming up gently tomorrow.

# Chapter 10

# Write Experiments: Edit

As you prepare to convert your shitty first draft into a good second draft and then a terrific third draft, I invite you to listen to George Saunders's wonderful video, *On Story*. He demonstrates a simple story changing entirely as he thinks about what each word means. He calls revision an act of love, which is a wonderful mindset for reading the next set of experiments.

There's a link to *On Story* in this book's resources.

# Write Experiment 17: Edit in Phases

## STORY: TEACHING OUR CHILDREN TO WRITE

My husband and I taught our children to write in phases. He explained to them that the first step is to make sure the content and overall structure are right. At this point, it is not worth worrying about whether the paragraph breaks are in the right places, the sentences are complete, or the words are spelled correctly.

Once the content and structure were right, we would move on to the paragraphs. Are the breaks in the right places? Is there a good topic sentence?

Only when that seemed about right would we suggest that they look at the sentences and words.

They found this frustrating at first because it seemed to drag the process out. They had written their papers and wanted to be done with them. But eventually they saw spending time fixing grammar and spelling in a paragraph that gets deleted is a waste of time. Neither one of them ever wanted to waste time while writing.

## OBSERVATIONS

Honor the editor in you. After finishing a first draft, invite the editor back to reshape and polish the raw material on the page.

First drafts are a necessary first step. Editing starts with judgments about the content, moves on to balancing the structure, and only then looks for the little distractors.

The very best books and articles are a pleasure to read on multiple levels. The information is enlightening, the stories illuminate the main points, and the sentences are clear and musical.

**STEPS**

1. Read through your whole draft without making any changes. Try to get a general sense of it as a whole. Does it feel complete and balanced? Make a few notes for later.

2. Do the editing experiments in order. While elsewhere I recommend skipping around looking for the experiments that appeal to you most, here I recommend proceeding through Write Experiment 18 through 22 in the order presented. They represent looking at the piece with a smaller and smaller aperture, from the whole to sections to paragraphs to sentences to words.

3. As you gain editing experience, you may choose to merge certain steps so that you don't have to make quite so many passes through your work.

4. Be aware that you may be opening and closing the aperture as you go along. A word that doesn't seem quite right may make you start considering whether the paragraph or even section really belongs.

**MORAL** Avoid searching for perfect words in paragraphs that may get cut later.

# Write Experiment 18: Edit for Content

## STORY: WHAT BELONGS?

Ji-Su is a fourth-grade teacher who likes to read aloud to her class. She reads not just the usual novel chapter on Friday afternoons, but also sections from their science and geography textbooks. She figures that some children learn best through their ears, so she tries to help them hear important concepts as well as see them.

Some of the textbooks are so full of words that Ji-Su wonders whether any of her students really read them. In her opinion, there is not enough content to justify reading all those words. There are a small number of ideas repeated over and over without much variation.

When that happens, she tells her husband, "That chapter would have made a good short essay. No wonder children have trouble picking out what is important."

Other times, there are so many ideas that her students feel overwhelmed. When she reads aloud, she tries to help them zero in on the key ideas and not get distracted by the other interesting but loosely related content.

When that happens, she tells her husband, "I feel like we are getting a complete mind dump from the author. How are the children to know what to retain?"

Somewhere in between is the sweet spot, where everything belongs and is expressed with just enough words to interest and illuminate.

## OBSERVATIONS

The goal of this phase of editing is to end up with just enough content, no more. The book or article has a central idea, and everything in the piece sheds light on it one way or another.

Writers generally know much, much more than they can fit into one book or article. Save some content for your next work. Many publishers prefer authors who know what their next book will be.

====== **STEPS** ======

Looking at your outline, book, or article, ask yourself the following questions:

1.  Does everything belong? If you did Write Experiment 1 in Chapter 8, pull out the notes you made about audience and purpose. Otherwise, it can be helpful to define criteria for inclusion and then evaluate each major idea against the criteria.

    • Who are you writing for?

    • What do they already know?

    • What do you want them to know when they finish your piece?

2.  Is there anything missing that is needed to make your piece complete?

3.  Should the piece be split into multiple pieces? I often find when I'm reviewing blog posts that there are multiple ideas supported by separate models or action lists. Why not publish each idea separately, perhaps creating a series and linking them together? In my opinion, one model per blog post is enough.

4.  Do all of the stories shed light on the main points you are trying to make?

5.  Are the stories told with enough detail to make them interesting without bringing in facts that are relevant only to you, not to your readers?

6.  Do you let your stories show your points without then telling readers what you meant? Showing is stronger than telling. If the story is well crafted, the conclusion will be clear without you telling your readers what they should have gotten out of it.

7. If your writing is aimed at behavior change, look at your balance of stories. Do you have a relatively even balance of stories about desirable behaviors, undesirable behaviors, and transitions? See Write Experiment 5 in Chapter 8 for more about story types.

8. If you are including humor to make your points, is it respectful and inclusive?

9. Does it make sense to summarize the primary points of a chapter at the end? Sometimes that makes a book easier to use as a reference. Some of my favorite self-help books end each chapter the same way, perhaps with a list of key takeaways or a set of reflection questions.

10. Particularly in a blog post, do you have a call to action at the end? This can be a single action that you recommend the reader take. It can also be a place to remind people that you have expertise and are available to help them.

---

**MORAL** Include just enough content, honoring your reader's time.

# Write Experiment 19:
# Cut Mercilessly but Save Your Outtakes

## STORY: AN IDEA JAR

James had a wise advisor in graduate school. When the professor saw that he was flitting from topic to topic because he had an over-abundance of ideas, she called him into her office.

"James, this is just a dissertation. Its purpose is to show that you can do original research and that you deserve your doctorate. It is not your life's work. You'll have many opportunities later to write papers on the topics that pop to the surface of your mind right now. What can you do to keep from being distracted every time a shiny new object emerges from your active brain?"

James's preschool son had brought home Adam Lehrhaupt's picture book, *The Idea Jar*, about children putting ideas for stories in a jar on the teacher's desk. That inspired him to find a large jar to put on the corner of his own desk. Whenever he had a new idea bubble up, he'd ask himself, "Does my dissertation really need me to develop this idea?" When he wasn't sure, he'd ask his advisor, who usually told him to put it in the idea jar. After he had written a short description of the idea and put it in the jar, he found he could let go of it. He knew he had captured it for a later time when he needed new ideas.

After he completed his degree, James used his idea jar over and over, not just when trimming a particular article or book down to size, but also whenever he needed to start something new. His slips of paper often inspired new projects.

## OBSERVATIONS

Part of editing is trimming content down to the essentials. But many people find it hard to delete sections that were hard work to write. To make it easier to cut what needs to be cut, plan to save your outtakes.

The writing that you remove does not have to be thrown away. The content that makes your blog post too long might turn into a separate blog post. The story or concept that you took out of your book might be an ideal topic for an online article that helps market your book. It might fit perfectly in your next book. In fact, it might suggest the theme around which your next book takes shape.

### STEPS

1. Decide how to store the stories and concepts that you remove from your writing as you edit at the content level. An actual idea jar may not work for long, since the pieces of paper are in random order. Perhaps you could use index cards organized in an index card box. Perhaps you could set up a section of your filing cabinet or a master directory on your computer. Then you can set up folders for particular topics and/or one folder for stories and one for concepts. This is similar to saving scraps of cloth from sewing projects to make a patchwork quilt.

2. As you edit, remind yourself that writing the pieces you cut was not wasted time. Even if you never use it again, a story or explanation that you remove may have led to the clarity of thought that remains in your piece.

3. As you cut, store any potentially reusable ideas in whatever you use as your idea jar. If paper files, attach a yellow sticky identifying the topic. If computer files, give them file names that will help you find them again later.

4. When you are at an impasse wondering what to write next, remember to consult your idea jar to see if you can find the seeds of your next piece.

**MORAL** Like a patchwork quilter, assemble leftover scraps into something new.

# Write Experiment 20:
# Edit for Structure and Order

## STORY: YOU LOST ME AT THE START

Back when I worked at IBM, a VP came to speak at a women's networking event. The only thing I can remember from her talk is her approach to emails: if she couldn't tell after reading the first sentence why she needed to read the email, she deleted it without reading any more. I imagine many people wondered why they never got responses from her.

That's why journalists learn the maxim, "Don't bury the lede." As people read the first paragraph of a newspaper article, they are asking themselves, "Do I want to read this article or not?" In case you're thinking I misspelled a word, the lede is the most newsworthy part of the story. Sometimes the maxim is stated, "Lead with the lede."

## OBSERVATIONS

I've heard similar stories told about blog posts. People read the first paragraph to decide whether it is worth reading the whole post. Estimates online for the average time people spend reading a blog post range from 30 to 90 seconds. Even if you take the high end of this range, there were many times when people spent less than 20 seconds before deciding, "Not for me."

A good start is important, but so is creating a structure that helps people understand your main points as you develop them. You might use the "Tell 'em what you're going to tell 'em. Tell 'em. Tell 'em what you told 'em" approach. You might start with a startling story and then tease it apart. While there's no single recipe, it makes sense to spend more time with your start and finish than you do with anything in between.

**STEPS**

Looking first at the whole piece and then at individual chapters of a book or sections of an article, consider the following questions:

1. Have you buried the lede and need to bring it forward? My own preference is to learn very quickly why I'm reading a particular piece of writing. Some people prefer a dramatic opening that creates an emotional springboard. That can work if the lede isn't too far behind.

2. Are your points in a logical order?

3. Does your conclusion follow naturally?

4. Is your opening strong enough that people will want to read on?

5. Are your units – chapters or sections – about the same weight? Could you explain the main point of each one in a single sentence? If not, you may be jumbling minimally related concepts together.

6. If you have several chapters in a book, do they clump together under major subtopics? If so, would it be helpful to have Part 1, Part 2, and so on?

7. Within chapters or blog posts, do you have section headers that help people see the structure?

8. Does your presentation make models or other structures clear and memorable? Sometimes a table is the clearest and most compact way to show the similarities and differences among distinct elements.

9. Remember the magical number seven, plus or minus two, a rough estimate of how many items people can keep in short-term memory at once. Do you have more concepts in the air than people can handle?

10. Because there is some evidence that odd numbers of items are easier for people to remember, can you make your lists consist of three, five, seven, or nine items?

---

**MORAL**  Clear structure makes ideas easier for readers to remember.

# Write Experiment 21:
# Edit Paragraphs and Sentences

## STORY: READ STRUNK AND WHITE

When I was in computer science graduate school, Dr. Fredrick P. Brooks held a class on writing for students who were working on dissertations and journal papers. He had a one-page list of instructions. The first item was, "Read *Elements of Style* by Strunk and White." The 10th item was "Read Strunk and White." The last item was "Read Strunk and White." That was good advice then, and it is still good advice.

One of my beta readers responded to the above paragraph with this caveat: "Some of the advice in Strunk & White is a bit outdated for today's modern writing style."

Language evolves. We are in the midst of a great transition with pronouns and pronoun agreement. When I was a child, the word *they* always needed a plural verb. Nowadays, *they* can optionally be a singular pronoun that refers to a person of any gender. That has been approved in various style guides for more than a decade.

There are times when the most effective way to make a point involves breaking one or more rules. But you can't make informed decisions about breaking rules without knowing the rules. If you break too many rules, then the times you do it intentionally are diluted.

———— // ————

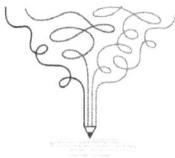

I once read that by 2051, the correct spellings of *it's* and *its* will be reversed. Today, *it's* is a contraction for it is, and *its* is the possessive of it. But apostrophes are slowly dropping out of contractions, and it would make more sense to use the possessive format for nouns. Watch for it.

## OBSERVATIONS

Clearly my list below cannot begin to cover all the elements of style. Even the very short Strunk and White is 85 pages long.

To give you a flavor of style considerations, I am going to include a few items that come up frequently when I am reviewing and editing.

## STEPS

As you read through your piece page by page, ask yourself the following questions:

1. Do all the ideas in each paragraph belong together? Many long paragraphs have two or more main ideas jumbled together.

2. Does each paragraph have a good introductory sentence and a good concluding sentence?

3. Are the paragraphs all a good length? Paragraphs that fill a page can intimidate readers. Very short paragraphs indicate emphasis. Use them sparingly. When writing for web articles, it is usually a good idea to have shorter paragraphs, since white space makes an online article easier to read.

4. Is your main point easily visible in either the beginning or the ending sentence? The first and last sentences in a paragraph are the prime real estate. You don't put your garden shed on the street as the first thing other people see. Is your first sentence like a garden shed?

5. Are your sentences easy to parse? Try reading a long sentence out loud. Do you have to back up and start over because you couldn't figure out where to put the emphasis?

6. Do you have any strings of words that aren't sentences? If so, did you write them that way on purpose, perhaps for emphasis, or would it be better to make them into full sentences?

7. Is there a pleasing variety of sentence structure and length? If all the sentences are short, the piece may seem monotonous. Longer sentences, particularly those that have a mix of dependent and independent clauses, require mental work to read. Are you considerate of the reader's time, making the value of the idea worth the work of deciphering your words?

8. Do you embed complicated side ideas in the middle of sentences? Often this shows up as words within parentheses. When readers have to put aside a partially completed thought temporarily because you've inserted a different thought in the middle of a sentence, they do not always reload the partially completed thought correctly.

9. If you use words that can serve as either nouns or verbs, do you provide clues so that the reader knows their functions without having to go back and reread sentences?

---

**MORAL** Give your readers the gift of a smooth, clear, flowing style.

# Write Experiment 22:
# Edit Words and Punctuation

## STORY: TOO MANY *ANDS* AND DASHES

As a writers' workshop facilitator, I used to find myself reading sentences that start with the word *And* with aversion. "And then I went into the building. And then I stopped at the counter." Back when I learned grammar, it was always incorrect to start a sentence that way. Had the rules changed without anybody telling me?

Realizing that this might be an area where the rules are changing, I started asking myself questions such as: "Is *And* adding anything to the sentence that isn't already there? Does it make the meaning clearer? Does it make the text flow more smoothly?" In my observation, it rarely contributed anything. That was just my opinion, of course.

There were other foibles that jarred me. People capitalize words that have no reason to be capitalized. They put words in quotation marks that aren't dialogue. Their prose is awash with exclamation points, parentheses, and dashes.

I got over my aversion when I remembered that I was reading early drafts. Opening sentences with a conjunction such as *And* or *But* or *So* (my personal habit) is very common in early drafts. So is connecting clauses with dashes and sticking side comments in parentheses. That's the way first drafts come out. When people are primarily focused on capturing ideas on paper, these habits of expression serve as lubricant, helping the ideas flow.

## OBSERVATIONS

Most exclamation points, opening conjunctions, parentheses, and dashes do not belong in a final version. If they are not edited out, they are like dancers wearing leg warmers in a public performance.

This final editing phase is about taking off any scaffolding that is no longer needed. It is about finding just the right word that can do the work of multiple words. It is about getting pronouns right. It is about subject verb agreement. It is about spelling and punctuation. It is the right time to remember Strunk and White's command to leave out needless words.

## STEPS

### Wording:

1.  Do you have precise words? Are all of them needed?

2.  Do you have adjectives connected with *and* that mean almost the same thing? Pick the better of the two, or find a word that encompasses the meaning of both.

3.  If you are using words in special ways, have you defined them before you used them?

4.  Have you checked words that have multiple spellings with different meanings to make sure you have the right one? Spellcheck may not find these errors. Examples include: to/too/two; there/their/they're; its/it's; peek/peak/pique; complimentary/complementary; principle/principal; whether/weather/wether. Well, maybe you'll never need to use wether, unless you have a sheep farm and need to write about castrated rams.

5.  Are you using slang or profanity? Some readers will not understand the slang, and some will be put off by profanity. But others will take slang as a sign that you know what is going on. Still others will view profanity as evidence that you are bold and direct. Know your audience and decide what works for them.

## Grammar including agreement:

1. In every sentence, do the subject and verb agree in all the ways they are supposed to agree?

2. Is the antecedent of every pronoun clear?

3. Have you decided what you're going to do about 3rd person singular pronouns (he/she, they, one, it) and are you consistent?

4. Particularly in books or articles about behavior change, have you decided how you are going to address the audience? You can include yourself by using we/our, or you can address them as you/your. Be consistent. It can be very confusing to have some sentences written in we-language and others in you-language. Sometimes people use we in the general discussion, but then use you in instructions. That's okay, as long as you are consistent.

5. Do you have split infinitives with an adverb in the middle? I usually try to avoid them: *to clearly state* sounds clunky and would be better said as *to state clearly*. Sometimes, though, a split infinitive can add emphasis. Is that helpful to the reader?

## Punctuation:

Most first drafts need a pass to remove quotation marks, parentheses, and exclamation marks.

6. Are you sparing with quotation marks around words? My preference is to use quotation marks only for quotations. If you are giving a word a special meaning, italicize it when you define it, and then use it normally. Do not use quotation marks to add emphasis.

7. Do you absolutely need any of the dashes that you've included? Would a period, semi-colon, or colon work better? Remember that colons serve as verbal equal signs signifying that what comes before the colon is the same as what comes after.

8. Can parenthetical remarks be either omitted or raised in status to their own sentences?

9. Do you use exclamation points too often? Like hot pepper, a little goes a long way. Writer Elmore Leonard suggests no more than two or three per 100,000 words of prose.

10. Do you want to use the Oxford comma: the comma that comes right before the *and* in a series? Whatever your answer, be consistent. Proponents believe it leads to clarity. Without it, the reader has to work a little harder to decide between two ways of parsing the words, as illustrated here: "This book is dedicated to my parents, Ayn Rand and God." Other people believe the Oxford comma is a waste of space.

This is just the start of polishing your text. I recommend rereading Strunk and White's *Elements of Style,* which contains rules of usage, principles of composition, and a list of words commonly misused. May your copy be as well-thumbed as my own.

The White of Strunk and White is E.B. White, author of the classic children's novel, *Charlotte's Web.* I can take advice from a man whose book has been enjoyed by so many children.

---

**MORAL**  Use elements of style that make writing vigorous and memorable.

# Write Experiment 23: Make Dialogue Clear

## STORY: WHO IS SAYING WHAT?

Stories make messages stickier. Dialogue makes stories livelier and easier to read. This is true not just for fiction, but also non-fiction that concerns humans and their interactions.

Jomo is a professional book reader. He used to read books out loud for the Talking Books series for the blind. That career evolved into reading books to produce Audible versions.

It makes Jomo grumpy when he finds people cramming an entire back-and-forth discussion into one paragraph. This does not happen so much in novels, where editors know how to space out conversation. But it happens with some frequency in non-fiction books that include stories. It makes him grumpy because he tries to alter his voice slightly for different characters in the conversation. Sometimes he has to back up and start over because he has lost track of who is saying what.

Jomo tells writers that they need to give him the right clues. The convention of a paragraph break between speakers helps him see that the conversational ball has crossed the net to the other side.

## OBSERVATIONS

Presentation matters. The way dialogue is laid out on the page and labeled can make it as easy and entertaining to read as your favorite novels. Cramming an entire dialogue into one paragraph or breaking it up in arbitrary ways can make it harder for your reader to keep track of who is saying what. It makes them have to work a little bit harder to follow the story. Whenever you make it harder for readers, you run the risk that they will think, "This isn't worth it," and put your piece down.

Looking at the overall presentation of a piece of work with the reader in mind is both a courtesy to them and a way to keep their attention.

There are some articles about writing effective dialogue in the book's resources.

=== **STEPS** ===

1. As you read novels, observe the way dialogue is handled. Is it easy to follow? Do you always know who is speaking? Look for the clues that the author gives you.

2. When you write dialogue, keep the speeches short. Only a very accomplished author can have someone give a multiple paragraph speech clearly. There's a particular way to punctuate such a speech. You include quotation marks at the beginning of each speech paragraph but leave out the closing quotation marks until the last paragraph. That is quite subtle and easy for people to miss.

3. Label the speaker in ways that add flavor. He said, she said, he said gets boring, though it is always an occasional option. It's better is to include something about the posture, voice, or intention of the speaker. Use words like *challenged* or *shrugged* or *stated firmly* instead.

4. Look at the way each speaker talks. Do the words match the speaker's personality? Does a forceful person use forceful words? Does a relaxed person use more easy-going words?

5. It is not necessary to label every speech item as long as you've established who starts, who responds, and then go back and forth. Perhaps label every third or fourth speech item so that people can be confident that they have not lost track of the speakers.

6. Read your dialogue out loud, trying to give different voices to the speakers. That might suggest ways to make it even clearer for your reader.

---

**MORAL** Make it easy for your reader to follow who says what.

# Write Experiment 24: Go Easy on Quotations

## STORY: TROUBLE WITH QUOTATIONS

Jason's book was copy-edited and ready to go to the book designer. Then his publisher dropped what felt like a bombshell: "You *have* acquired permission for all the quotations, haven't you?" Jason had a quotation at the beginning of each chapter and several more scattered through the text. It had not occurred to him that he might need permission to quote other people's work. He even had one exercise that used an adaptation of somebody else's questionnaire.

His publisher suggested that he contact an intellectual property lawyer to make sure he was safe from legal action. Jason ended up paraphrasing most of his quotations and attributing the idea to the original author. For three quotations, he contacted the publishers to obtain permission to use the exact words and paid the prices they stipulated. His book needed more proofreading to make sure he had not introduced errors replacing quotations with paraphrases.

Janet's story is different. She submitted a piece to a writers' workshop with this quotation attributing it to Maya Angelou. "I've learned that people will forget what you said, people will forget what you did, but they will never forget how you made them feel." One of the reviewers challenged her to identify where Maya Angelou said or wrote this statement. Consulting a quote investigator, she found that a version of this statement can probably be attributed to Carl W. Buehner, a high-level official in the Mormon church. Janet had seen this quotation on placards all over the Internet. But none specified where it was published. The BBC even ran an article in 2017 titled *Let's Save Maya Angelou from Fake Quotes* in response to this and other misattributions.

## OBSERVATIONS

Copyright law protects authors from having others use their words without attribution or recompense. As an author, appreciate that before becoming frustrated that it may stand in your way. Popular wisdom suggests that an author can include quotations up to a certain word limit, but that's not always so, especially with song lyrics and poems. Anything published before 1927 (in 2022) is in the public domain. Fair Use Doctrines specify some criteria against which a copyright infringement case will be considered in court. A copyright covers the expression of the idea, not the idea itself, which is why Jason's approach of paraphrasing was safer for him. He included attribution out of respect to the people whose work inspired his words. Where his work was a direct extension of somebody else's work, he played it safe, acquiring permission, which sometimes cost him money.

Janet, who misattributed her quotation to Maya Angelou, now takes anything she sees in quotation collections or placards on the Internet with a large grain of salt. The very freedom that makes it easy to publish online leads to some fast-and-loose misquoting, with no publisher to ask about permissions.

When I read pieces heavily laden with quotations, I feel that the authors are giving away their power. Why not make their own statements, instead of relying on somebody else's words?

## STEPS

1. Whenever you feel the urge to include a quotation, ask yourself the following questions:

    - Could I say this in my own words as a reflection of my own expertise without calling on someone else's words?

    - Could I paraphrase and give the original speaker credit for the idea? Copyright covers the expression of an idea, not the idea itself.

- If I need to quote someone either to inspire or illuminate, do I know where the quotation originated? Can I find the source, perhaps by consulting a quotation investigator?

2. If a quotation is really important, determine whether you need to acquire permission to use it. You may need to pay for a license. Copyright rules are complex and different in different countries.

——————//——————

While editing this book, I removed many quotations of recent authors. For the Anne Lamott quotation at the beginning of Chapter 9, I purchased rights to use it from her publisher because I thought she made the point perfectly.

MORAL When in doubt, leave a quotation out.

# Write Experiment 25: Include References Deftly

## STORY: JUST ENOUGH, NO MORE

Justine wanted to turn her master's thesis into a popular book. That took some doing. A thesis is very formal. It is structured for academic readers who want to know where everything came from. They expect a serious review of the literature and every point to be backed up thoroughly. They know how to read text that is littered with citations.

Justine was lucky enough to have honest friends. One told her, "When you have all those citations, it looks like you have nothing to say for yourself. Why would I read your book?"

Another said, "All those citations make it feel too much like being back in school."

Still another said, "Yeah, but if you're going to say, 'Research says something,' I want to know whose research. All research isn't created equal. Some of it is crap."

## OBSERVATIONS

Here are the beliefs that shape my reference preferences in writing for the general public:

Some don't care at all about the background research. They should not be distracted or burdened with in-text citations or footnotes.

Some are meticulous about checking up on my thinking, or they are just plain curious about the research. They should be able to follow my references relatively easily.

I strive to have enough confidence to own my own opinions. Thus, including source information is a service to the reader, not a chance to drop names. Unless the source adds something to the discussion, I may choose not to use it.

Online articles are an interesting case because people know that they can turn any text into a link to something else. As a reader, I particularly dislike this approach because it takes me away from reading the article while I'm still in the middle of it and because I don't know where the links will take me. I'm a suspicious person. I want to know before I click that I'm being taken to an article or book.

*Table 3: My Preferred Reference Approach for Online Publications*

| Approach | Mention the author in the text in a natural way and then include a reference list at the bottom of the article alphabetized by author's name. |
|---|---|
| Example | "As Hammer and colleagues demonstrate, we unconsciously adapt to tacit workplace norms…" This is not linked, since that would take people away. The reference to the Hammer article is included at the end of the piece. This is linked, if possible, to an online resource. |

*Table 4: My Preferred Reference Approach for Books*

| Approach | Include an Endnotes section that refers back to chapter and page and gives additional information that the user might want. These endnotes can also include discussion that would otherwise break the train of thought in the chapter itself. Think of it as a gift to the especially curious. |
|---|---|
| Example Endnote | Chapter 1 p. 27: The VIA character strengths inventory was developed by Martin Seligman and the late Christopher Peterson. Character strengths are measured by an online assessment. For a list of many research articles about character strengths in various settings, see [include link, or remind people that you have links on a website supporting the book]. For a list of books about VIA strengths, see [link]. |

Finally, a reminder that we all need periodically: when you use a source, capture the information about it right then, even if you're not sure you are going to include it in your references. Otherwise, you may have a hard time tracking it down later.

**STEPS**

1. Consider your likely readers. Are they curious about your sources or do they prefer to take your word for it? Keep this in mind as you decide what sources to include and how to reference them.

2. You could follow my preferences, or you could look through other books or articles to find an approach that feels natural to you. Sometimes particular publishers have standards that you will need to follow.

3. Capture your sources as you go. My recommendation is to use a tool where you fill in data fields, such as author, title, publisher, journal, and year. These tools generally produce reference lists in multiple formats, taking care of details such as punctuation and italicization that can be very tedious to get right. Examples include the Microsoft Word source management tool and various online tools. A Wikipedia article on reference management lists more than 30 tools.

4. As you write, keep asking yourself, "Will any of my readers want to know how I know what I'm saying?" For example, you need to identify the researchers whenever you find yourself writing, "Research shows" or "A study indicates."

5. Remember that a big shot's opinion is worth no more than yours, though sometimes it may seem more convincing.

===== **STORY CONTINUED:** =====

Justine decided to include endnotes with discussion of sources followed by a reference list in APA format. At the last minute, her publisher told her the references needed to be in AMA format. She was very glad she had them in a tool that supported both formats.

**MORAL** Make your sources easy to find but unobtrusive to honor all readers.

# Write Experiment 26: Read Aloud to Yourself

## STORY: WHAT DOES IT SOUND LIKE?

I read many books aloud to my husband. I often wish authors had read their books aloud, usually when I read halfway through a sentence and then have to start over because I made a wrong assumption about the way the words worked together.

Consider the word *present*, which can be a noun, a verb, or an adjective.

"I got a present on my birthday."

"Present company is excluded."

"I present my case."

They sound different when said aloud, particularly the last one. But if I can't tell quickly from the context and sentence structure which meaning is intended, I may find myself putting stress in the wrong places. This can be avoided if the author provides clues such as punctuation to make the different meanings instantly apparent.

Then there is the matter of how the words sound. Even people who read to themselves tend to hear the music of the text or lack thereof in their heads. Does it sound jerky? Does it have a sing-song quality? Does it drone? Or are rhythm and sound patterns clear and pleasing?

I have read aloud all the books I've written or edited. I do it when I feel that a piece is ready for prime time. I almost always find small mistakes that missed my eyes earlier.

Many of my friends only read books by listening to them read aloud, including one friend who has a waterproof player and ear buds and takes books along on her two-hour swims. Reading aloud helps you think about how people will experience your words via their ears.

## OBSERVATIONS

Reading aloud helps you see places to make your prose even more eloquent because:

- It slows you down. The average rate of spoken English is 150 words per minute. The average rate of silent reading is 200 to 250 words per minute.

- You involve hearing as well as sight. Does the sentence sound good when you hear it?

- As you translate from visual text to spoken language, you are meeting your readers halfway, seeing the pitfalls they may encounter. It gives you a chance to be compassionate.

- You will see things that your eyes have been skipping over during earlier proofreading.

- If you choose later to read your book aloud to produce an audiobook, you will thank yourself for taking this step. Audiobook publishers tend to insist that you read the book word-for-word as it appears in print, so it's better to catch the hard-to-read sentences now while you can still change them.

## STEPS

1. Read your piece out loud.

2. As you read, listen to the words coming out of your mouth. Ask yourself the following questions:

   - Does it ever sound choppy or monotonous? Perhaps there are too many short sentences or perhaps all the sentences are constructed alike. You could try varying the sentence structure or putting some of your short sentences together into longer sentences.

- Do any sentences seem like they will never end? Do you feel like you have to stack up so many ideas in your mind that you fear you'll lose track of some before a sentence is over?

- At the points that seem like natural pauses, do you have appropriate punctuation such as periods or commas?

- Do you ever find yourself making a mistake about the meaning of a word (like *present* in the story) such that you have to backtrack and start over?

- Are there any missing or extraneous words? These sometimes happen when editing a sentence using cut and paste.

3. If you edit anything, be sure to read it out loud again. When it sounds smooth and flowing, good job.

4. Particularly for short pieces, some people suggest reading it sentence by sentence starting from the end and working toward the front. That's more than I ever do, but it is one way to make sure you aren't missing anything.

---

**MORAL** Use your eyes and ears together to polish your prose.

# Chapter 11

# Moving from Write to Share

## Wrapping Up the Write Experiments

All of the experiments in the Write section can help you get the actual work of writing done. Perhaps you have used some Imagine experiments to fill your head with the ideas that you want to capture. Perhaps you have used some of the Draft experiments to go from fuzzy ideas to a rough draft ready to be polished. Perhaps you have used some of the Edit experiments to revise until you feel you cannot make the words any better. For a quick review, Table 5 contains the morals from the Write experiments:

Table 5: Collected Morals from the Write Experiments

| Write# | Category | Moral |
|--------|----------|-------|
| Write 1 | Imagine | Your audience wants only a small fraction of everything you know. |
| Write 2 | Imagine | A playful spirit welcomes new ideas and new ways to arrange them. |
| Write 3 | Imagine | Break a big project down into manageable steps. |
| Write 4 | Imagine | Reach into your life-long well of experiences for inspiration. |
| Write 5 | Imagine | Collect stories as you see them occur. |
| Write 6 | Imagine | Concepts may be easier to carry around in the brain than stories. |
| Write 7 | Imagine | New writing can emerge from old documents and pictures. |
| Write 8 | Draft | Use either the accelerator or the brake, not both at the same time. |
| Write 9 | Draft | Find a way to turn attention from the fear of writing to the work. |
| Write 10 | Draft | Even being blocked can be a launchpad for writing. |
| Write 11 | Draft | A little bit of writing every day can get a lot done. |
| Write 12 | Draft | A well-chosen structure makes both writing and reading easier. |
| Write 13 | Draft | Writing about daily routines is capturing history in the making. |
| Write 14 | Draft | Talking can become writing. |
| Write 15 | Draft | A lost document may still be in your head. |

| Write# | Category | Moral |
|--------|----------|-------|
| Write 16 | Draft | Plan today for warming up gently tomorrow. |
| Write 17 | Edit | Avoid searching for perfect words in paragraphs that may get cut later. |
| Write 18 | Edit | Include just enough content, honoring your reader's time. |
| Write 19 | Edit | Like a patchwork quilter, assemble leftover scraps into something new. |
| Write 20 | Edit | Clear structure makes ideas easier for readers to remember. |
| Write 21 | Edit | Give your readers the gift of a smooth, clear, flowing style. |
| Write 22 | Edit | Use elements of style that make writing vigorous and memorable. |
| Write 23 | Edit | Make it easy for your reader to follow who says what. |
| Write 24 | Edit | When in doubt, leave a quotation out. |
| Write 25 | Edit | Make your sources easy to find but unobtrusive to honor all readers. |
| Write 26 | Edit | Use your eyes and ears together to polish your prose. |

Now it is time to involve other people as collaborators, reviewers, publishers, and readers.

# Introduction to Share Experiments

Writing is a communication activity, but it is often performed in solitude. People think of writing time as lonely time. Sounds contradictory, doesn't it? This section of the book contains experiments to help writers make the writing process more social.

There are sixteen experiments in this section. To make them easier to navigate, I have organized them into four categories:

- **Audience**: Tailor writing to the audience you want to attract as readers. See your own writing as other people see it.

- **Support**: Set up accountability structures involving collaboration, co-working, and feedback.

- **Publication**: Prepare writing to reach the desired audience, whether in book, article, or blog form. There are many choices involved in navigating publication effectively.

- **Network**: Get other people to help spread the word about published works. If nobody knows about it, nobody can benefit from reading it.

# Why Sharing is Important

People are better at keeping promises to others than they are to themselves. Having an external deadline is crucial for people who don't (yet) love writing for its own sake. Otherwise, writing is often considered important but not urgent, and thus stays on the back burner. Sometimes with practice, people get over the dread of writing and grow to look forward to the time spent writing. Until then, deadlines such as commitments to reviewers keep them practicing.

People do not necessarily see what is strong in their own writing until other people point it out. Recently, one writer was amazed to hear that the short draft that she disparagingly called "a last-minute bit of something," prompted a reviewer to say she was a great writer. Reviewers can help a writer see the gems that should be kept, whatever else gets cut or altered while editing.

People may give lip service to the idea that they should seek brutal reviews, but most people don't really want them, and they don't know how to use such negative feedback. In order to absorb feedback, people need to feel that they are safe. Creating a safe and honest place to share reviews is the point of the writers' workshops described in Chapter 13.

Being honest does not have to mean diminishing the writer. In really good reviews, readers can help writers see where their audiences are likely to misunderstand the intended message, where they bury the lede, where their argument misses a step, where their words lead astray. They humbly submit suggestions for making pieces even stronger while acknowledging that the piece belongs to the writer, who is free to take or leave their suggestions. Sometimes two reviewers disagree about a suggestion, a great reminder that readers are not all the same and nobody knows it all.

People often think the first draft should be good to go, so they are nervous about asking for reviews on early drafts. However, seeking feedback early helps writers invest their writing effort more effectively. Why not test the overall shape and effectiveness of a piece before investing time to polish it? One of the advantages of collaborating with others is that people see other people's writing in the making. As they see the value of the feedback they give others on early drafts, they become more relaxed about offering their own drafts for review.

## Helping Others Can Help You

Writing is a skill that gets better with practice and paying attention. What is surprising is that paying attention to somebody else's writing builds the reviewers' skills as much as paying attention to their own writing. When reading a piece multiple times to prepare to summarize the key takeaway, point out the strengths, and make suggestions, people see things that otherwise might get past them: new ways to organize, new ways to use vibrant language, new ways to hook the reader, new ways to cite research to make people curious, new ways to end on a strong note.

# Reaching Your Audience

Writing for yourself is fine, but most people want to make a difference in the world with what they write. That means publication. Today there are numerous options for publication, some with no gatekeepers to prevent access. You can self-publish books or blogs, or you can submit them to various publishers and publication services. There are hybrid options where others help you self-publish. The options can be bewildering.

Once the work is published, you need to get the word out that it is available. Unless people know about it, they won't read it. That is when it is helpful to take stock of your own network and the networks of the people in your network.

The overarching moral for all of these experiments is to let other people help you become the writer you want to be.

# Chapter 12

# Share Experiments: Audience

Writing is for an audience. It may be an audience of one, your best friend or even your future self. It may be people close to you who share your history and culture. It may be a broader audience that includes people who are very unlike you. To share with them effectively, spend some time thinking about what they need and what they already know. Do your part to make the dance between writer and reader graceful.

# Share Experiment 1: Picture Ideal Readers

## STORY: IMAGINING READERS AROUND THE TABLE

Let's return to the story of John Yeager started in Write Experiment 1 in Chapter 8. He pursued his goal of writing a book for sports coaches by interviewing more than 50 coaches, people whose performance had impressed him. He asked them questions about the ways they handled the issues that sports coaches tend to face and the relational skills that helped them develop individual athletes and build strong teams.

Besides numerous ideas and stories that enhanced his book, John gained a strong sense of his ideal audience, including the questions that occupy their attention and the practical limits on what they can do. Every person he interviewed had struggled with at least some of the topics he raised. Every suggestion in his book had been used effectively by somebody he interviewed.

———————— // ————————

In a similar way, this book is based on my own experiences with writers. I feel like I have many writers sitting around a large imaginary board room table, ready to advise me when critical questions arise and to tell me where I'm getting off track. For example, one writer told me point blank that this is not a book for writers of fiction. I don't have any experiments to help writers develop characters or escalate plots. She reminded me that the writers I know mostly write non-fiction, and in fact, they mostly write to change the world. Her voice is just one of the voices in my head that keeps me focused.

## OBSERVATIONS

In an TEDx talk titled *Quantum Physics for 7-Year-Olds*, physicist Dominic Walliman argues that scientists can learn to explain their science to non-scientists. Drawing from his own experience, he listed four principles for communicating effectively with non-experts. The principle most relevant here is to start in the right place. Establish a connection to something that the audience already knows and use terms that they already understand. You can find a link to the video in this book's resources if you are curious about the other principles.

That raises the question: How do you know where to start? If you are speaking to a person or group, you can ask questions.

"We're here today to talk about quantum mechanics. How many people know what we mean by quantum mechanics?"

If anybody says no, start by explaining very clearly using analogies to things they already know. Those who know a little bit already will probably appreciate the review.

When you're writing, you can't ask questions to determine the best starting place. That is why it is important to have a good picture of your ideal audience and to keep checking what you are writing against your mental images of what they understand.

## STEPS

1. Do some thinking about explaining your ideas for different audiences. I suggest watching some of the videos in a series by Wired Magazine in which experts are challenged to explain the same concept to a 5-year-old, a 13-year-old, a college student, a graduate student, and an expert in the field. There's a link to a playlist of these videos in this book's resources. In each video, a real expert explains an idea to a real person, so you can see how the explanations land. Notice how different the explanations need to be.

2.  Describe your ideal audience, the people you most want to read your writing. Pertinent questions might include:

    •   What is their education level? This allows you to check that the reading level of your book is appropriate.

    •   What are their primary interests?

    •   What is their existing comfort with your subject?

    •   Where do they go for fun, for shopping, for social connections?

    •   What makes them curious?

    •   What keeps them up at night?

    •   What would bring them to your writing?

3.  If you can, think of four or five real people who fall in this group to be on your advisory board. These can be people whose needs you want to be sure you meet. Perhaps they are classmates, colleagues, clients, or members of your congregation, social club, or family. Anybody who has said they really need your book is a candidate.

4.  If you cannot think of enough real people, imagine some. Give them faces and personalities and make sure they are outspoken and willing to tell you what they think.

5.  When you find yourself needing to make decisions, bring your imaginary advisory board to mind. Imagine what they would tell you about the question at hand. If they are real people, you can sometimes actually ask them, but you might keep that for the most important questions so that you don't wear them out. You will probably have a good sense of the way they would respond.

————//————

I initially included demographic questions about gender, geography, age, and race in the questions listed in Step 1. A beta reviewer cautioned me to tread carefully. Research indicates that using demographic information to identify a target market reinforces stereotyping. She suggested instead focusing on patterns of thinking, beliefs, and emotions.

**MORAL** Imagine advisors who can speak for your ideal audience.

# Share Experiment 2: Find the Sweet Spot

## STORY: LOST IN THE DETAILS

Jacqueline wanted to write a book about a particular topic that she had been studying for more than 20 years. She had looked at her subject from several viewpoints, and she had tried out various ways to understand what she observed. She likely knew more about the topic than anyone in the world. She had been deepening her understanding for a long time.

When she shared early chapters of her book, she found only her very best friends would read it all the way through. Even they confessed that they got lost in the details.

I suggested that she put herself in the shoes of her readers. What did they want to know more about? What would make it worth their time to read her book? She did not have to please everybody. Some people would never be interested in the topic. But to reach her ideal audience, she needed to know what would make them curious enough to stay with her book.

## OBSERVATIONS

Figure 4: The Sweet Spot

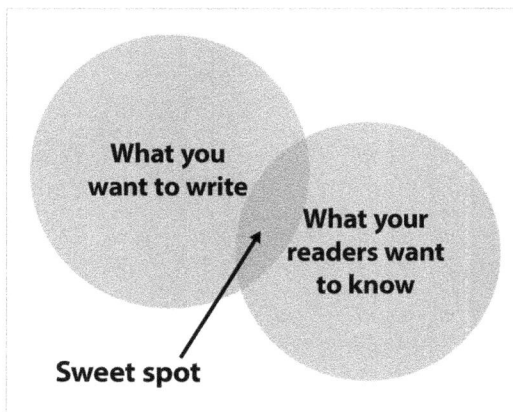

I have made this point before at least twice (see Write Experiment 1 in Chapter 8 and Write Experiment 18 in Chapter 10), but it may be that this is the experiment that will help the idea stick with you.

Nancy Ancowitz wrote some ideas for helping people prepare for online meetings. She shared a simple Venn diagram that I have adapted here. Her point was that speakers needed to refine their messages to connect with the needs of their audiences.

To write effectively, it is important to know your subject. But that is not sufficient to make a compelling book. You also need to know what your readers want to know more about. What makes them curious? What are they searching for when they pick up a book? Do they want to solve particular problems? Try on different ways of feeling? Distract or entertain themselves? Find role models for future growth?

Once you've done some serious thinking about the intersection between what your audience wants to know and what you want to write, you'll be prepared to make the many small decisions that go into deciding what belongs in your book or article.

## STEPS

1. Make a copy of the Venn diagram to post by your writing station as an ongoing reminder that just because you want to write it does not mean your audience wants to read it. This may help you stay in the sweet spot.

2. If you are writing about something you feel passionate about, tell the reader about your passion in the introduction or author biography. Here are some prompts that may be helpful:

   • Where did the passion come from?

   • Why is the subject so important to you? Why are you called to write this piece?

   • How long have you been involved in the topic, and how did your interest start?

- How has thinking about the topic affected the course of your life? Often people write about topics they need to know themselves.

3. Make a list of questions that might draw readers to your book.

4. For example, to write about a woman that you admire, you might have these questions:

   - What did she do that was so amazing and how did she do it?

   - How much of what happened was her and how much was luck?

   - How has she been able to survive some very hard times?

   - What mistakes has she made and how did she recover?

   - What impact has she had on the world?

   - If I wanted to be more like her, what would I do?

   - What can we expect from her going forward?

5. Here's another example, questions that you might ask if you were writing a self-help book:

   - When are the approaches described here useful?

   - Who is most likely to benefit?

   - What changes does this approach help people make?

   - Who has tried it and what results did they have?

6. You are not obligated to answer all the questions your audience has. The sweet spot is the intersection of the two circles, not the union. You may choose to tell them in the introduction what you are not going to do, setting out the boundaries of the sweet spot for their benefit as well as your own.

7. Use the questions you have defined as your criteria for deciding what belongs and what does not. When editing or planning your outline, you can hold up certain topics against the list of questions your readers care about and ask yourself, "Which question does this help answer?" If none, that might mean that you're missing a question and need to add it to your list. Another possibility is the topic you're considering may have stimulated your thinking but it does not belong in the finished book.

---

**MORAL**  Some ideas are like wall studs, supportive but not needing to show.

# Share Experiment 3:
# Check for Cultural Sensitivity

## STORY: DEFAULT SETTINGS

I wrote the story in Sit Experiment 1 in Chapter 3 based on a real experience in a writers' workshop. The writer had been given some advice about how to describe characters vividly, including a suggestion that she read Russell Baker's book, *Growing Up*, for examples of exquisite description. A friend read my story and responded thus:

"As for the anecdote, I have a suggestion. The writer you feature seems to be in the default setting of white. I'd love to see her show up in your story as more potentially of African descent since she was from Africa. To someone like her should go the credit of acting vigorously on a good suggestion. Why do I say default setting of white? Because blue eye color is given prominence in your anecdote. It was interesting to me that even though almost everyone Russell Baker described was of European descent, our writer had no trouble taking the general point and applying it to many descriptions of African people."

Good feedback. I rewrote the story in my experiment leaving out blue eyes.

## OBSERVATION

I found the following useful definition of cultural sensitivity in a presentation by the New York City Human Resources Administration. There is a link in the book's resources.

*Insert 9: Cultural Sensitivity Definition*

1. Being aware that cultural differences and similarities exist without assigning them a value – positive or negative, better or worse, right or wrong.

2. Being aware that cultural differences and similarities exist and have an effect on values, learning, and behavior.

3. A set of skills that allows you to understand and learn about people whose cultural background is not the same as your own.

Humility helps us better reflect cultural sensitivity in our writing. It fosters alternative perspectives and curiosity as we strive to understand how words will land with our audiences. Cultural sensitivity can lead us to think seriously about whether our words make any of our intended audience feel left out. For example, if all our stories and statistics come from the United States, do we intend to neglect an international audience? If not, how can we make our content more inclusive?

Cultural sensitivity also leads us to consider whether we are appropriating another group's culture in an inappropriate way. This is not to say that we create tight swim lanes where only people with Italian ancestry are allowed to talk about pizza. We are in a world where ideas, styles, and artifacts are flowing in all directions. The English language is made up of words absorbed from all around the globe. But it does mean avoiding superficial or thoughtless references to concepts that others find worthy of reverence, such as powwow, rain dance, and totem pole. It means giving credit to the sources, even asking for permission.

Cultural sensitivity also involves checking colloquialisms that may give offense. There are some good lists online of terms to avoid. Cultural competence is a way of showing respect.

**STEPS**

1. Review your envisioned audience. The questions in the previous two experiments may help you sharpen your mental picture of the people you want to reach with your words.

2. Go through your stories and examples one by one. What identifying information have you included? Is it needed to make the story interesting? Are there ways you can make the story vivid without narrowing the applicability?

3. Look at your entire collection of stories as a whole. You might want to capture your list of stories in a spreadsheet along with information about the characters. For each story, indicate relevant identifying information. See Figure 2 in Chapter 8 where I identified gender. Whatever your criteria, look at the balance. Are there groups that you want to reach that seem excluded? What can you change that would help your collection be appropriate for your entire audience?

4. Read through your book or blog looking for cultural references. Look for references to rituals, slang, clothing, food, and any aspect of life that varies from culture to culture. For each, ask yourself:

   • Do I know enough to use this?

   • Am I using something lightly that people in the culture would treat seriously?

   • Will it sound natural coming from me?

5. Look for slang that may be offensive to some of your readers.

6. If you are unsure about the appropriateness, either check with somebody belonging to that culture or just leave it out.

**MORAL**  Cultural sensitivity broadens your audience.

## Chapter 13

# Share Experiments: Gather Support

*"...we with our lives are like islands in the sea, or like trees in the forest. The maple and the pine may whisper to each other with their leaves.... But the trees also commingle their roots in the darkness underground, and the islands also hang together through the ocean's bottom. Just so there is a continuum of cosmic consciousness, against which our individuality builds but accidental fences, and into which our several minds plunge as into a mother-sea or reservoir."*

~ William James, *Confidences of a Psychical Researcher* in *The American Magazine, Vol. 68 (1909)*

Writing does not have to be a lonely activity. How can you involve others effectively in your writing process?

# Share Experiment 4: Try Coworking Arrangements

## STORY: WORKING IN TANDEM

Jonquil had a lot of trouble focusing on her writing while working from home. There were so many distractions. She could fix a snack or start a load of laundry. On her laptop, she could visit Instagram to catch up on her friends. She could look through book recommendations on GoodReads. She could watch funny videos or news clips on YouTube. She could shop for shoes or summer clothes. Endless attractions were just a few finger clicks away.

Taking a walk with a close friend, she bemoaned her inability to get work done. Her friend knew exactly what she meant because they shared the same inability to stay focused on work with all the eye candy on their laptops.

Together they decided to turn peer pressure to their advantage. They made a date to meet at a local coffee shop, one that had no problem with people sitting for long periods working. After saying hello and buying coffee to justify using the space, they set a timer for 50 minutes. Each settled down to work.

Jonquil told me that she was ashamed to open YouTube or Instagram with her friend close by. They both focused on the completely unrelated tasks that each had on the top of her list. When the timer rang, they each bought a fancier coffee and visited for 10 minutes before setting the timer again. The next break, they agreed they could each open Instagram for 10 minutes.

Jonquil and her friend repeated this way of working as often as they could find available times to get together. Both felt it was exactly what they needed to stay on track.

People feel ashamed to open games or social media in their workplaces because it's clear that those activities are not part of work. Who knows who might walk up behind them without warning? But there are many reasons not to go to workplaces, including long commutes, irregular hours, and during the pandemic, risk of infection.

Working at home removes that direct social pressure to stay focused on work. It can also be lonely.

Brad Neuberg started the coworking movement because he wanted to be able to work on his own and still have the advantages of social contact at work. His movement has resulted in thousands of coworking spaces being established around the world. Generally, people become members and then share the space, furniture, and utilities while they work on separate ventures. In case you're interested in starting a coworking space, you'd have Neuberg's blessing. He invites people to take his idea and make it their own.

Coworking doesn't have to involve a special space. Some people meet in coffee shops. Some meet on Zoom, opening the working time with a brief check-in, then each going about their separate tasks knowing they can talk or ask questions.

———————— // ————————

This experiment focuses on supportive relationships between peers who help each other stay on track. Working with a writing coach can be a different kind of supportive relationship in which you set goals and watch progress together. A coach can be a confidential partner who helps you strategize, track progress, figure out ways around obstacles, and celebrate successes. The magic of coaching is the way new perspectives bubble up in conversation.

**STEPS**

1.  Start with **Who**. Do you have friends who also need to make progress toward particular goals and want help avoiding distractions? Or perhaps you know people who get lonely working at home and want some regular interaction?

2.  Decide together **Where**. In a coffee shop? From home via Zoom? Is there a coworking space in your area that you could join? Would you like to start a new coworking space?

3.  Decide together **When**, including how often. Do you prefer ad hoc meetings or a regular schedule?

4.  Decide whether you want to use a timer to break up work time into periods of concentration and periods of socializing or relaxation. If you are in a coworking space, this may require too much alignment among participants. But if you are on Zoom or in a coffee shop, it can demark periods of concentration from periods of socializing and relaxing together.

5.  Consider opening a timed coworking session by asking all participants to state what they intend to accomplish. Then set the timer and go.

6.  Consider closing a timed coworking session by reviewing progress as well as discussing what worked well and what you'd like to change in future sessions.

**MORAL** It is easier to be accountable to someone else than to yourself.

# Share Experiment 5:
# Consider Having a Co-Creator

## STORY: TO PARTNER OR NOT TO PARTNER

I have co-created several books with equal partners, and I found most experiences extremely rewarding. I am using *co-creating* to include both co-authoring and co-editing.

In the book, *Smarts and Stamina*, the key idea came from Marie-Josée Shaar. I helped create the overall shape of the book, and I contributed many of the stories and activities. When we were finished, each of us had probably touched every word in the book, which benefitted from our different styles and viewpoints. I gave her the final say on most disagreements.

My next experience was co-editing *Character Strengths Matter* with Shannon Polly. I learned so much from her about acting "as if" to develop strengths. Without her, the book would not have had the poems, speeches, and stories for people to read aloud to act "as if" they were brave, kind, humble, and so on. There was so much work that it was a blessing to have someone to share the effort. We had some tussles, but those usually made the book better.

I am writing *Sit Write Share* by myself. It is my idea, and I have nobody that would be an equal partner in its production. When I want feedback, I have my writers' workshops. The work is also so much fun that I don't need to share the load.

People sometimes have co-creating arrangements that do not work well. Jolene had a partner who made big promises but barely delivered, submitting work of such poor quality that it could not be used. It was very hard to have that person's name on the title page after the stress of redoing the work.

Jian spent a lot of time arguing with his partner, finding they had different ideas about the direction of the work, without any clear means of resolving disagreements.

Jovia was shocked to find out she had given up intellectual property rights for her own ideas by contributing them to a book.

## OBSERVATIONS

Whether or not to find a partner depends on the balance between benefit and cost. For me, the balance has been different in different situations. I have seen creativity emerge from the space between people, such that afterwards neither person knew who really had the great idea. When this happens, co-creating is immensely rewarding.

But there are pitfalls that can lower trust and cause downright suffering.

Attention to the quality of the relationship is important from start to finish. Take a leaf out of the contract lawyer's book. The work of a good contract lawyer is to keep people out of court by spelling out terms ahead of time. Think about the terms of a co-creating arrangement before getting too far into it. Create and sign a written agreement to keep everyone involved clear about what was discussed.

## STEPS

1.  As you start on a major writing venture, here are some questions to help you decide whether taking on a co-creating partnership would be appropriate:

    •   Is there more work involved than I want to do by myself? Would it be worthwhile to share the work with someone else?

    •   Would I benefit from having a creative sounding board who is also intimately involved in the project?

    •   Am I lacking expertise in some areas important to this project that another person could provide?

    •   Is there somebody available that I would enjoy working with?

    •   Would a partner help with the marketing of the product?

    •   Would we be broadly equal partners, or would some other arrangement such as requesting a guest chapter be more appropriate?

2. Assuming you find someone to work with, take time to work out the terms of the agreement to protect yourself from future distress. The remaining steps suggest topics to include in your agreement.

3. Recognize that conflicts will arise and discuss how you will resolve them. Does one person have greater decision-making authority? Will one person make the final decisions in one part while the other does so in another part? Or will you keep hammering out a disagreement until you reach consensus?

4. Decide how you will handle expenses, credit, and profits. Whose name goes first on the author list? Alphabetical order is neutral, but any other order implies that the first author is primary. Are expenses and royalties split evenly, or does one partner take more of the risk and/or get more of the payback?

5. For any ideas that either person submits, are there restrictions on the way that person can use those ideas going forward? Does the person have to ask other authors for permission to use stories, concepts, or tools in later works?

6. If one partner does not perform adequately, what recourse does the other have? Will it be possible to remove the person from the author list and restrict the person's share of the royalties? How will this be decided? Is there anyone else who needs to be involved to decide if this is appropriate?

7. Write down your agreement. Make sure you agree on the terms. Revisit it periodically to see if you need to change anything.

———————— // ————————

Concerning managing conflicts, Marie-Josée had the final say for *Smarts and Stamina* because the book was her idea. With *Character Strengths Matter*, Shannon had the final say on the act "as if" segments, and I had more say in the essays we selected.

**MORAL** Spell out an agreement today to prevent future heartache.

# Share Experiment 6:
# Find a Good Writers' Workshop

## STORY: FEEDBACK DOES NOT HAVE TO BE BRUTAL

Listening to a broadcast interview of several writers, Joshua got the message that he should seek brutal feedback, so he joined a group that prided itself on giving exactly that.

While he didn't find it too difficult to give harsh feedback himself, he did not find it particularly satisfying to get it. He would leave workshop meetings thinking, "Why didn't they get it? Didn't I do anything right? I just don't have the energy to fix it."

When he heard somebody say, "Feedback should be viewed as a gift," he wondered if maybe there were other groups in which feedback could actually feel like a gift rather than an opportunity for others to be witty at his expense.

Joshua kept looking. He was lucky to find a workshop run on the principles described in the next experiment. After a few months, Joshua wrote the group leader, "I love working with the Writers' Workshop! I've gotten so much out of it. I'm better at giving and receiving feedback, and my writing is getting stronger."

## OBSERVATIONS

It is true that we all need constructive feedback that helps us see where we can get better at the craft of writing, but we also need to know what already works. An exclusive focus on what is broken deprives us of the reinforcement we need when our words are true and clear.

Many writers get together regularly with other writers to take turns reviewing and commenting on each other's work. In my experience, a very structured approach that focuses as much attention on what's strong as on what could be stronger tends to work better than an open-ended free-for-all. It's easier for reviewers to prepare comments, and it helps the writer build courage and confidence. Workshop members often call it a safe space to experiment.

Looking for strengths works better in a group. Sometimes I go into a workshop not particularly bowled over by a piece, but other people's comments about strengths make me see it in a new light.

It's easy to see what's in it for writers. They get to observe the way their pieces are received, hear the strengths spoken out loud, and receive specific suggestions for improvement. But what's in it for the reviewers? They build their writing skills by paying attention to the way other people write. They recognize things done well, and they pick up new ways of expressing what they mean. If they struggle to understand another's piece, they become more aware of the need to support the understanding of their own audiences. They also get to see works in progress, which helps them accept the imperfections of their own early drafts.

## STEPS

1. Look for an existing workshop or create your own (see the next experiment). You can find anything on the Internet. University writing programs may have open groups. There may be notices in local libraries, coffee shops, or local social media about writers' workshops seeking members.

2. Try out a group with your emotional feelers alert.

3. Did the feedback open your mind or make you cringe? When you left, did you feel energized to revise or discouraged?

4. Was attention paid to the strengths in the writing as well as possibilities for improvement?

5. Did people seem genuinely interested in connecting with the work or were they more interested in showcasing themselves?

**MORAL** Seek a writers' group that can give balanced feedback.

# Share Experiment 7: Run a Writers' Workshop

## STORY: HERE'S HOW I DO IT

In this experiment, I describe the way I run workshops and why this approach works. This could be useful to you whether you are starting a workshop yourself or want to provide quality feedback as a reviewer.

Aren Cohen wrote the following words based on a comment she made in a workshop review of this experiment. She thought I was being too modest.

*Insert 10: Joining a Writers' Workshop*

> Becoming a writer is hard. Becoming a **good** writer is even harder. Joining a writing workshop is an excellent idea, but writers' groups can be a mixed bag. Groups can fall anywhere between empowering and disabling. Setting intentions, ground rules, goals, and guidelines are essential for making sure that the time spent in the workshop, both as a writer and a reviewer, is fruitful.
>
> In 2006, I had the extremely good fortune of befriending the remarkable Kathryn Britton. Seven years later, I became even luckier when I joined one of Kathryn's very first writing groups. At the time, I had gotten stuck with my writing. I trusted that Kathryn would have a thoughtful, organized, and constructive approach to her workshop that would help me rebuild my courage as a writer. She did.
>
> In an ideal world, everyone would join one of Kathryn's writing workshops! However, since Kathryn is a mere mortal, we cannot clone her. Luckily, Kathryn is an extremely generous person and willing to share her secret sauce. While it may be impossible for you to join a group led by Kathryn herself, one of her key intentions for this book is to empower others to learn and lead by sharing her best practices.     ~ Aren Cohen

I include a story after the steps to illustrate this way of running writers' workshops.

## OBSERVATIONS

The approach described in this experiment is one that I've been using with a few tweaks for more than eight years, successfully reviewing more than 3000 pieces of writing. Most pieces have been some form of non-fiction, but we have also reviewed short stories, novels, poems, song lyrics, website copy, TEDx scripts, marketing brochures, college applications, and of course, all the experiments in this book.

A writers' workshop is a regular meeting of writers who take turns reviewing and commenting on each other's work. The approach I use is based on Richard Gabriel's wonderful book, *Writers' Workshops & The Art of Making Things*. He made his book available online after it went out-of-print.

Over time, I've experimented with group size and ways of organizing the delivery of comments. I conduct all my workshops online and record sessions so that people can listen to the comments again when they are ready to revise. The steps below are a good start for both creating a workshop yourself and also understanding what a balanced workshop could look like.

Assume a group has assembled. My groups tend to be three or four people with a separate facilitator who does not have work under review. This creates a nice balance between having enough voices to get a good range of comments and having turns often enough to make the workshops worthwhile. With a group this size, it takes about 30 minutes per piece to complete the process.

## STEPS

1.  Settle on shared intentions concerning how much ahead of time people need to submit. Also discuss how the group wants to handle late submissions. In my groups, it's accepted that reviewers owe no apologies to writers for not having comments for a late submission.

2.  **Start by setting the stage**. Ask the writer to introduce the piece very briefly. Who is the audience? Where will it be published, if at

all? Remind the writer not to tell the group what the piece is about. Reviewers will do that in Round One of the review. Ask the writer to read one paragraph from anywhere in the piece so reviewers can hear it in the writer's voice.

3. **Ask the writer to become a fly on the wall.** That means the writer steps out of the circle and doesn't speak again until the end of the review. In an online workshop, writers mute sound and turn off the camera. Stepping out of the circle liberates writers to listen. Instead of needing to explain or defend the writing, they can hear how other people experienced it.

4. **Round 1 – ABOUT:** Reviewers take turns describing how they experienced the piece. These observations can be short summaries, statements of the major theme, or discussions of emotional impact. They are usually brief, and several reviewers may say roughly the same thing. If everybody takes away the same message, that's great, as long as it was the message the writer intended. If not, the writer got some important information.

5. **Round 2 – STRONG:** Reviewers take turns answering the question, "What makes this piece of writing strong?" These comments can be at any level, from the clarity of the overall argument to well-chosen words or phrases. Reviewers might comment on the theme, the story arc, or what gave the message power. They may read aloud particular sentences that they found eloquent. Here are some questions to help people see strengths:

   • What really worked?

   • What did I really like?

   • What would I keep no matter what else changes in the piece?

   • What parts do I remember best?

6. I have found it works best to call on each person to give a top strength and then to open the floor for free-form discussion. This means that reviewers think ahead of time about the priority of their comments. It also means nobody speaks too long at once. When I used to ask people for all strengths at once, the discussion was much less interesting, and the last speakers often felt everything they had to say had already been spoken.

7. **Round 3 – STRONGER:** Each reviewer answers the question, "What, in my opinion, would make this piece even stronger?" That gives reviewers the chance to do what we all expect to do in reviews: add value by suggesting changes. Notice two things about the question. First, "in my opinion" is a reminder to both the writer and the reviewer that the writer can take or leave the comment. Second, the question is about making it even stronger. Somehow that wording makes it easier to hear the comments because they are not pointing out what's broken, but instead suggesting ways to make something already strong better.

8. Similar to the discussion of strengths, I call on each reviewer for a top suggestion and then open the floor for discussion. In addition, I often remind people to stop after two or three suggestions, lest the writer be overwhelmed. Particularly when people are submitting early drafts, I also try to remind reviewers not to focus on minor details such as spelling mistakes that will be caught during editing. We tend to call these *twinkies*.

9. Invite the writer back into the circle to ask questions for clarification. Since the writer can't talk during the review, this is the time to get things cleared up. Remind the writer not to explain or defend the writing.

10. Thank the writer, and then turn attention to the next piece.

## STORY: A WORKSHOP IN ACTION

Joshua brought an 850-word blog post about renovating a bathroom to a group that I was facilitating. All workshop members had read it ahead of time to prepare comments.

When I asked him to introduce it, he said, "I want to publish it on my home improvement blog." Notice that he did not tell us what it was about.

In Round 1, he heard people summarize what they were taking away from the piece. "This piece was about steps to take before starting a home improvement project," or "This piece gave me a confidence boost to start working on getting my bathroom renovated."

In Round 2, he heard what other people felt were the strengths of the piece.

Good feedback is very specific to the work. Contrast "Great post," to "The way you demonstrated how to choose between different kinds of flooring was so clear and sharp that I'll print it out to keep for the next time I remodel any room in my house."

The focus of good feedback is on the writing, not the writer. Contrast "You are a great writer," to "The way you opened the post made me curious. I often skim the first paragraph and decide not to keep going, but you hooked me right at the start."

Perhaps most important, the feedback offers insight into what's good. Approval is great, but Joshua needed to know how the approval was earned so he could do it again. Contrast "You know a lot about home improvement," to "You showed me how to sort through my ideas, who to get involved, and how to be sure I will still like my renovation after a few years."

Joshua was surprised to hear strengths in his piece that he didn't know were there.

When the discussion of strengths wound down, we went on to Round 3. Once again, I asked each person to give a top suggestion for making it even stronger, and then we opened the floor to general discussion.

Two reviewers disagreed about one point. One really loved the opening, and another felt that it took Joshua too long to get to the point. It's fine when that happens. Joshua will have different readers who will not all agree. He gets to decide which feedback he takes. When people started getting into spelling and grammar errors, I reminded them that Joshua told us that this was an early draft, and that he will take care of those details in a later revision.

Finally, we invited Joshua back to ask questions for clarification. He didn't quite understand a particular suggestion. When he started to explain something that a reviewer found confusing, I reminded him of our rule: no explanations or defenses allowed. He can take or leave any comment made by the group. We don't have time to be told what he meant it to mean. Either we saw it, or he has work to do.

---

**MORAL** A structured review works better than a free-for-all.

# Chapter 14

# Share Experiments: Publish

There are many options when it comes to publishing. You can send your writing to your family and friends in a holiday letter. You can publish on your own blog or create videos of you reading aloud. You can submit to existing magazines, newspapers, and online publications. You can self-publish or find a publisher.

How do you navigate all of these options? What's the best form of publication for you? Perhaps these experiments can help you find your way.

# Share Experiment 8: Blog

## STORY: SOME LIKE IT SHORT

Jacques was building a business. His specialty was coaching millennial entrepreneurs through the bumpy waters of getting ideas launched, staff assembled, and money invested. He had an excellent track record with the people he helped, but he wanted a broader audience. Some of his clients suggested he bottle his secret sauce in a book, but that held no appeal. He just didn't have the time to fuss with pulling a book together and then selling it. Frankly, he didn't believe his ideal readers had time to read books.

One afternoon, his assistant, Jori, made a proposal. She liked writing much more than Jacques did. She pointed out that the Internet provides wonderful opportunities for reaching like-minded people. How about starting a blog with short articles that his clients could read in less than five minutes? Jacques was willing to try it.

They scheduled a meeting every Tuesday morning. Together, they talked through a few interesting ideas and then settled on one. Jacques listed key points to be made. Jori wrote it up, got a quick review from Jacques, and then published it by noon Wednesday. Most of the posts were fast reads with lots of white space. Jori found pictures on no-royalty services to make each blog post pop.

As hoped, the blog started attracting new business. People subscribed, adding themselves to the email list Jacques used to announce new offerings. Jori tweeted about each article to gain a wider following.

## OBSERVATIONS

Anybody can publish online. If you publish completely on your own, it may take time and a lot of work to get a following, which will probably depend on the size of your network and how much your articles match the needs of the time.

Running a blog on your website can be a good way to build business, attracting eyes to the product or service you offer. Articles can showcase your expertise, your personality, and your passions.

**STEPS**

1. If you want to build some confidence before you start your blog, evaluate online sites that publish articles on topics that you find interesting. As editor for *Positive Psychology News*, I have helped many writers interested in positive psychology get started. We edited their articles, published them for our readership, and posted them on social media. Although we held a copyright on the articles so we could syndicate them easily, we gave authors permission to reuse their articles freely, for example, in their own newsletters, websites, or books. Be sure to understand the rules before you submit.

2. If your purpose for writing is to build an audience of people interested in your business offerings, explore publishing articles on LinkedIn. While it may have started as an online Rolodex for keeping track of people wherever they wander, it has become a major tool for business building. There are right ways and wrong ways to use it that are beyond the scope of this book. Do some research, starting with references listed in this book's resources.

3. Medium.com can be used as a blogging platform, but it also hosts a number of publications that can expand the readership that sees your posts. They all have their own rules and desired content.

4. If you decide to run a personal blog, write several articles before you post the first. Many bloggers post one or two articles and then stop, building no momentum. Having enough articles ready to keep your blog going at a regular rate for several months is important for building a readership.

5. Use keywords and hashtags to attract people who may not already know you. Use social media to share and gain readers.

6. There is no perfect length for blog articles. Some like them short, some like them longer.

   • Shorter than 300 words is probably too short, since search engines penalize *thin* content.

- Several online bloggers suggest that Google tends to prefer content rich websites. Medium published an article in 2015 on internal research indicating that articles that capture the most attention take seven minutes to read. At around 250 words per minute, that is roughly 1700 words. There are relevant articles about article length in this book's resources.

- You could try running an A/B test, publishing the same content in different length versions to see which gets more hits, comments, and social engagement.

7. Remember that readers probably do not read longer articles word for word. They tend to scan the beginning, look for a list in the middle, and then read the end. Don't put your most important content in a long paragraph in the middle.

8. Illustrate your blog posts with at least one image that fits the message. As you look for pictures online, be aware that just because you can find it does not mean you are free to use it. Look for sources that say images can be used with attribution. There are some sites listed in the resources. Be sure to include the attribution in your post.

9. Consider producing VLOGs or video logs. Write your content, practice it a few times, and then record yourself speaking. Upload to Vimeo or YouTube, and then embed your videos on your website. YouTube has built-in editing software so that you can trim unwanted information. Some people prefer watching and listening to reading, and it is one way to give people a sense of who you are. LinkedIn search rules have changed to give preference to video content over written pieces.

**MORAL** There is more than one way to become a published author.

# Share Experiment 9: Freelance

Jada wanted to make her living writing. She started by publishing short articles on Medium.com. When she learned that Medium supports various channels for more targeted publications, she started submitting her content to ones that covered topics she found interesting. She established her eligibility to get paid by gaining 100 followers. Whenever she published a new article, she clicked the meter-my-stories box. She sent the following message to her friends:

"I also wanted to share that I made my first $0.04 from Medium, almost a whole nickel!!! I will actually write a short piece on that too - but I feel like framing it!!!! I couldn't be more excited about a payday!"

Jada decided to get serious and started sending pitches to newspapers, magazines, and online blogs that accepted outside articles for publication. She sent a lot of pitches before she got her first response, but she persisted. She also refined her ability to track what readers would find interesting. She understood it was all about clicks for the editors. When she published a short article in the *New Yorker*, she was over the moon. Now she was a true freelancer. She built up a portfolio using the online tool Muck Rack, which automatically updated her list of publications whenever she published a new article. With her dynamic portfolio, she found it easier to get editors to read her pitches.

Her friend Juma made a living watching football (soccer) on television and writing two or three short articles every day for online magazines around the world. When asked if he were ever out of work because football was out of season, he laughed, "Football is played around the world. It is always in season somewhere."

## OBSERVATIONS

People can earn a living with freelance writing. Some learn how to sense what is hot in the moment and submit pitches that pique the interests of busy editors. Some find companies that need web content on a particular subject. Some ghostwrite articles or books. Much of this is outside my expertise, so I spoke to a young friend, Susannah, who is both a freelance writer and a copy editor for the *New Yorker*. She has worked on both sides of the story.

Susannah said the way most freelance writers she knows make a living is by publishing in a number of blogs and print publications that cover their beat, that is, the area of interest and/or geography they want to cover. Some have broad beats, while others are more narrowly targeted, like Juma. Many start out working in editorial or administrative roles and then start pitching their own pieces.

Rates for publications vary widely. If they accept your article but end up not publishing it, many editors will pay a kill fee. You can then submit the article elsewhere.

When I asked Susannah what she most liked about freelance writing, she said she enjoyed getting responses from both friends and strangers regarding the pieces she had published. She also appreciated watching her articles become even better in the hands of a good editor. We agreed that is a great way to build skill.

If you are seriously interested in this option, there are many resources online to help you learn the profession. Check the resources accompanying this book for some examples.

**STEPS**

1. Decide on your beat, that is, your area of interest. Will it be broad or narrow? How does it connect with what people find interesting right now?

2. Identify a story you are interested in writing. Make sure it has a hook, that is, something that will interest readers and keep them interested. Then email a pitch to the editors of the relevant sections of multiple publications. That means doing some initial research:

   • Find a peg in order to get the pitch through the door. A peg is a currently happening reason for publishing the article right now. It could be an important news story or social trend or time of year. Editors will be wondering, "Why will people click to read this article right now?"

   • Form your own hierarchy of desirability for different publications. Some may be higher in prestige or pay scale. Pitch to them first. If you do not hear back within a few days, move down your list. Your list may include not just print journals but also online-only publications, such as websites with very active newsletters.

   • Check to see if something very similar has been published recently in a chosen publication. That will not be a good publication to target.

   • Read the instructions for submitting for each publication that you want to pitch. Many publications have a page on their website or information in the masthead that specifies submission guidelines, what sections are supported by freelancers, and the word count for each article type. Many accept submissions through a contact form.

   • Find out how to email the editor in charge of the relevant area. If you know someone on staff, ask about the right editor. Look to see if editors at the publication have active Twitter presences that reveal their interests. You can always email the primary editor and hope that your pitch will be forwarded to the right area. But getting there directly removes one chance of your pitch getting lost.

3. Conventional wisdom says that it is bad practice to submit the same pitch simultaneously to two publications. However, that is more important for people who have established themselves than people who are starting out. It is also important if you have a big scoop. As a beginner, it is okay to send most pitches to multiple editors. For full transparency, include in your pitch, "I have also reached out to [name] at [publication]."

4. Write a good pitch that will get a second look from editors. They often get more pitches than they know what to do with. Here are possible elements of a good pitch.

   • Subject line: "Pitch for story on [two-word subject description] referred by [personal connection name]."

   • A pitch should be no longer than a short paragraph, four or five sentences at most.

   • Introduce yourself. If you have a personal connection to the editor, mention it in the subject line and the first line. "I am a writer on [name your beat] whose material has appeared [in what publications]. I got your name from [contact]."

   • Sum up the story in no more than two sentences. "I have a story about [topic]." Just hit the highlights: the main topic, what it is pegged to, and how much reporting you have done for it.

   • Include the word length of the article as it stands. Indicate whether it could easily be cut or extended to meet length requirements of the publication.

5.  Things may move very slowly or very quickly. It is a good idea to have a draft ready when you pitch so you can respond quickly if given a short deadline.

6.  Do not include the actual article until they express interest.

7.  Build a portfolio of your articles as you publish them. If a potential client wants evidence that you can write, you can tailor your portfolio to show you understand their needs. Look for online tools that can help you maintain your portfolio.

---

**MORAL** With persistence, it is possible to make money writing.

# Share Experiment 10:
# Explore Book Publication Options

## STORY: WHERE DO I GO FROM HERE?

Over a long and illustrious career as an educational coach and consultant, Jasper had helped thousands of parents and teachers navigate important challenges with children in school. Often his clients said, "You should write that down so you can help people who can't be your clients." Or they might say, "Write that down so that I can remember it the next time I have to face this challenge." When he finally got around to it, he produced more than 60,000 words of stories, suggestions, and activities. Some of his activities were based on handouts that had always helped his clients make progress. Jasper felt he was achieving his mission to ease the way for parents and teachers facing the same challenges his clients faced.

Jasper went to a conference on publishing nonfiction and was chagrined to hear a speaker say that it was a rookie mistake to complete a manuscript before finding a publisher. He heard the speaker say that he should have shopped a book proposal to publishers when he had just a chapter or two completed. That way the publisher could have a say in what he wrote.

When he talked to a few book agents at the conference, they asked him how large his platform was. "I have about 1000 people on my mailing list," he said with some pride. They let him know that 1000 names did not represent a particularly impressive list. A publishing house is in the business of making money by publishing a book. No matter how wonderful his material, they need solid evidence that it would sell before they could invest money bringing it to market.

Publishers also wanted to know what Jasper could do to sell it. Would he go on book tours? Participate in podcasts? Hire a publicity firm?

Thoroughly disheartened, Jasper looked for other options. Should he pay to publish it himself? Would that mean a garage full of books and many trips to the post office?

Then he learned from a friend that self-publication has substantially changed over the last 20 years. Doing it himself would get the book published quickly, and he could call all the creative shots for cover and interior design.

It took Jasper about five months to take his book from a computer file to a published paperback and e-book. He hired a book advisor who guided him through the steps. After revising the book based on beta reader comments, he sent it first to an editor and then a proofreader. He worked with designers to achieve a cover and interior design that looked professional. The book advisor helped him navigate all the details of book publication. It took time, effort, and money for the support services, but he was very happy to launch his book to the entire world.

Around the same time, his friend, Jennifer, was invited to pitch an idea to a textbook publisher. They had put out the word that they were looking for a textbook on a topic that was dear to her heart. Jennifer had been publishing articles on her topic on LinkedIn, where she had a large following. Impressed by her pitch, knowledge, and facility with social media, the publisher gave her a contract to write the book and then supported her through the entire process. Jennifer believed that she would never have finished the book without the deadlines her executive editor imposed regularly. Her editor also allayed many of her recurring fears, "Do I know enough? Will anybody care? Will there be any readers?" The editor told her that practically every writer had similar fears.

## OBSERVATIONS

The publishing industry is no longer the solitary gatekeeper to the readers of the world. People can now publish books themselves that look and feel like books from traditional publishers. They can also make them available to people around the world through various online bookstores. Self-published books can be hard backs, paperbacks, e-books, and audio books.

Each book author needs to make an informed decision about route to market. The brief summary of publisher and self-publication advantages in Table 6 may help you get started on your decision.

*Table 6: Advantages of Publisher and Self-Publish Options*

| Publisher Advantages | Self-Publish Advantages |
| --- | --- |
| There is a substantial cachet to getting a book contract with a well-known publisher. To many people, the publisher's name on the title page is social proof that the book is worthwhile. Somebody thought it was a good bet to publish it. | You have control over all of the creative decisions that go into your book. With a publisher, you may not even get to choose your book title. One friend despised the book cover design from his publisher, and they told him he could only make small changes. |
| The publisher shares the risk, paying for cover and book interior design and editing. They expect to make money to pay back these expenses. | Your book generally gets to market more quickly. You aren't held up waiting until the publisher feels it is the right time, given all the other books they are publishing. A publisher typically takes nine months to two years to bring a book out. |
| The publisher may provide the deadlines and encouragement you need to finish. | You do not have to spend time writing a book proposal and shopping it to agents and publishers. |
| The publisher often has a staff of experienced designers and editors so you do not have to vet that talent yourself. | You select the people who do the design and editing, which gives you some additional control. |

| Publisher Advantages | Self-Publish Advantages |
|---|---|
| The publisher may give you a book advance (later counted against royalties) that can help cover the time you spend finishing the book. | You can update your book whenever you want. |
| A publisher's editor may help you stay focused on finishing the book. | It's clear who owns the content. |
| A publisher has established pathways into bricks-and-mortar bookstores and libraries. | You receive a higher percentage of the royalties. |

Before we go on to how to make the decision, consider the wisdom of Chip and Dan Heath in their book, *Decisive*. They suggest that whenever you have a binary choice, a good first step is to expand the options. Using a publisher comes in a wide array of choices, from the big names to specialty houses to university presses to boutique firms that target specific topics or audiences. Are there any that might be interested in your subject? With self-publishing, you can do it by yourself, or you can hire a professional such as Jasper's book advisor to guide you through the steps and make decisions.

When do you look for a publisher? If you intend to seek a publisher for a non-fiction book, it is probably a good idea to start submitting your proposal and query letter when you have all of the components of the proposal gathered, which includes an outline and sample chapter. You may need to write more of the book to clearly determine the contents and structure. Different publishers ask for different levels of content control, so waiting until you have a complete manuscript is not a fatal error, but you may need to work harder to respond to their feedback.

Be aware that with either traditional publishing or self-publishing, you will be instrumental in marketing your book. Getting a publisher to create your book does not mean that you have delegated the marketing to them. They need evidence that you have the energy and means to reach your target audience. After a few months, their attention will go on to the next project.

STEPS

1. Lay out your options, trying to have more than two, but not so many that you feel paralyzed by too many choices. Perhaps consider three to five options.

2. Review the advantages of all your options. You could start with the information in Table 6 and then do some additional online research. I just skimmed the surface. Check the resources accompanying this book for some additional information.

3. Ask people you know who have published using any of your routes. What were their experiences? Would they do it again the same way? What would they like to change?

4. If you can find them, and it's not easy, talk to some potential agents to get a clear sense of whether they think your book is a good candidate for a publisher. You can often find agent names in the acknowledgments of books like your own, or you may have people in your circle who could introduce you to their agents. You can also search for agents online. Agents help people find publishers and negotiate contracts.

5. Once you've made up your mind, change your focus from "What is the right decision for me?" to "How can I make this the right decision for me?"

---

**MORAL** Find the route to readers that works for you.

# Share Experiment 11: Find a Publisher

## STORY: TIME TO WRITE A PROPOSAL

Janelle decided that she wanted to publish her book with a well-known publishing house. She believed her book, tentatively titled, *Work at Home Without Going Crazy*, would be relevant to many people long after the coronavirus pandemic of 2020-2022 faded into the past. She believed there were many people who would never go back to the office full-time and that they would benefit from her suggestions and enjoy her humor. Janelle had been writing online articles for years, and she had a substantial LinkedIn following.

Janelle bought a good book on writing book proposals and started filling in the blanks. She struggled with shifting her attention from what she most liked about her writing towards what would make a good business case to a publisher.

She looked through the acknowledgments in several business books on her shelves to find the names of possible agents. In her mind, authors who liked their agents would thank them publicly. She asked a LinkedIn contact to introduce her to an author who then introduced her to an agent. The agent agreed to read her draft proposal.

Finding the proposal full of both potential and holes, the agent gave her mountains of feedback to make a stronger case for the book. After Janelle made the updates, the agent started shopping it to publishers. Many turned it down rapidly. Janelle laughed that she put her rejections in her freezer and she was running out of space for ice cream. Finally, two publishers showed interest. Janelle let her agent manage the negotiations with the publishers, figuring the agent knew more about reasonable terms than she did. When her book was published with a major publisher, she figured her agent had earned 15% of the proceeds that he had negotiated on her behalf. He also pushed her to start thinking about her next book.

**OBSERVATIONS**

Publishers are businesses. They publish books because they believe they can make money. To find a publisher, you have to be convincing that your book idea will attract buyers and that you have the ability to deliver it.

If you are not particularly strong at self-promotion, you can learn to get better at it. You can also outsource some of the work. For example, a literary agent represents the business interests of writers. If you hire a literary agent, you are exchanging some of your future profits for their expertise, time, and contacts. When it comes to negotiating a contract, they may be able to demand higher returns than you can imagine asking, or they may help you reduce any unreasonable expectations you have.

Different publishers have different niches and different business cases. A book proposal may represent a market that is too small for one publisher while it fits the needs of another publisher exactly. An agent may be able to help you find your way to the right publisher.

**STEPS**

1.  Get a good book or online resource on writing book proposals. These resources can help you learn what information should or should not be included and how to format the proposal so that you look like you know what you're doing.

2.  Put yourself in the mindset of making a business case for your book. You have to convince publishers:

    •   The topic is timely and will sell to a large audience.

    •   The quality of the main book idea is something they can be proud to publish.

    •   You are the right person to write the book.

- You write well, and you will get the book done.

- You have a platform already established that will bring the book to the attention of a large number of readers.

3. Describing comparable titles serves two purposes: It shows the publisher that there is an existing market, and it shows how your book adds something unique and valuable.

4. Consider finding an agent. On the one hand, agents must be paid for representing you. Typically, agents receive between 10% and 20% of the proceeds they negotiate for the author. Recognize that you are paying for expertise that you do not choose to develop for yourself, for time that you do not want to invest, and for contacts you do not have. Particularly if you are uncomfortable promoting yourself, a good agent may get a better contract than you would get for yourself. Agents often give practical feedback on book proposals, which helps authors build better business cases. Some agents *may* help people put rejections in context, helping authors handle disappointment.

5. Treat all that you meet on the way to publication with consideration. Respect their time, remember that their reasons for being involved are different from yours, and respond quickly when they make requests of you. You are not your agent's only client. Agents and publishers may talk to each other. Be the kind of person that your agent finds rewarding to represent.

**MORAL** You can outsource some work to a literary agent or publisher.

# Share Experiment 12: Publish Your Own Book

**STORY: SELF-PUBLISHING MILEAGE VARIES**

This story is about my own experiences with self-publication.

In January 2007, Senia Maymin decided to start *Positive Psychology News*, an online publication with almost daily articles about positive psychology in action. Soon after, I joined the effort as managing editor.

In 2009, we decided to collect 16 articles from the site into a book that we called *Resilience: How to Navigate Life's Curves*. This was very much a do-it-yourself endeavor. I selected the articles, got permissions, and invited Kevin Gillespie to draw black-and-white illustrations. When we were happy with the draft, I generated a PDF file in the right format for a 5.5 by 8.5-inch paperback. I uploaded the file to Createspace, Amazon's self-publication service at the time. Then I used a Createspace template to generate a cover with a picture purchased online. The book was only 122 pages, just too thin to have the title on the back spine. We fixed that later by publishing a second edition with one more article.

We published a sister volume in 2010, *Gratitude: How to Appreciate Life's Gifts*, using a similar homespun process. Both books are still for sale on Amazon. We have sold more than 800 copies of *Resilience* and over 300 copies of *Gratitude*. That's more than the 250 copies that the average self-published book sells in a lifetime, but it is not stellar.

In 2015, I joined forces with Shannon Polly to publish the third book in the Positive Psychology News series. We once again invited Kevin Gillespie to illustrate, and we asked the author of each article to agree that the royalties would go to the Christopher Peterson Memorial Fellowship at the University of Pennsylvania to support scholarships for the Masters of Applied Positive Psychology program that most of the authors had attended.

Things were very different this time: Shannon had a cover designed by a graphic artist. We vigorously sought endorsements. We launched the book at the International Positive Psychology World Congress in 2015. We continue to market the book energetically during speaking and consulting engagements. Shannon sends a copy to each of her coaching clients. We frequently remind people in the positive psychology community that the book exists and that the royalties honor Christopher Peterson, one of the giants in the field.

We also pushed for Amazon reviews. *Resilience* has two reviews. *Gratitude* has three. *Character Strengths Matter* has 92. The more positive reviews, the higher the book will rank in Amazon searches and the more often it shows up as a similar book.

Finally, we published *Character Strengths Matter* in three formats: kindle, paperback, and audible. At this moment, *Character Strengths Matter* has sold more than 7200 paperback, audible, and kindle copies. We have contributed more than $46,000 to the Christopher Peterson Fellowship Fund. In his column on self-publication, Tucker Max considers 5000+ sales over five years a home run. But it is still less than the 10,000 that traditional publishers consider a non-fiction success. Not every book they publish is a success, of course. In his process, Max aims for 1000 sales over the first three months because that indicates a momentum that keeps word of the book spreading.

With *Sit Write Share*, I have decided to self-publish again, mostly because I do not want to make promises to a publishing house about how much money and effort I will invest to market it. I prefer to have only myself to please or disappoint. I remembered that one of my peers promised her publisher that she would hire a publicist to help her get the book in front of people. That is an option I am considering.

However, I expect to apply the lessons from *Character Strengths Matter:* I will have professional cover and book interior designs. I will get somebody else to edit it. I will ask for endorsements and Amazon reviews. I will organize a launch team who know my work and are willing to speak up about my book. I have hired a book professional to steer me through the unfamiliar steps.

## OBSERVATIONS

There are many activities involved in publishing a non-fiction book successfully that go beyond writing and editing your own words. You have to understand how to get your book in front of the people most likely to read it. You need to acquire ISBNs. If you want to have hard cover versions and feature in bookstores, you need to publish with different services instead of or in addition to Amazon. Your cover and book interior need professional design. You need to involve others to help you sell it. You need to ask for endorsements and feed content to a launch team. After the book is published, it helps to participate in podcasts and interviews to advertise your expertise, reminding people that they can get your book to learn more.

You do not have to do this completely on your own. There are professionals who call themselves book shepherds or book advisors who know all the steps, have good contacts for professional services, and have probably solved the main problems many times before. There are book marketing services that can help you spread the word.

## STEPS

1.  If you are reading this experiment seriously, you have made up your mind to self-publish. Now it is time to make self-publication the right decision for you. I suggest thinking seriously about what success means to you. Whatever your reasons, understand how self-publication can contribute. Here are some options to consider:

    - Will it give you credibility with your usual clients?

    - Will it help you gain bigger speaking engagements, podcast invitations, or radio interviews to spread your ideas?

    - Do you want books to give away or sell to event audiences?

    - Do you want to reach some people in a profound way, even if that audience is too narrow to be tolerated by publishing houses?

    - Do you want the book to support a training program that you will deliver in your area of interest?

- Do you want to be able to update your book frequently to stay current with a fast-moving field?
- Is your book your legacy?

2. Consider hiring a book professional who can help you navigate the complex dance it takes to complete a book and bring it to market. My book advisor, Diana Needham, has given me a long list of to-dos to take this book to market. She has arranged the list on a timeline with estimated due dates for certain activities. She knows the order in which they need to be done and how long before publication each needs to be completed. Finding a book professional is like finding a general contractor to make renovations on your house. Ask around, get references, and check with other people who have used their services.

3. If you don't hire a book professional, make a to-do list yourself for getting your book completed. Insert 11 includes some of the items for your list. They are only in rough order, and you may not choose to do all of them.

4. Look at the list and honestly mark the activities that you really do not want to do for yourself. For many of these activities, such as designing a book cover and formatting the book interior, it is unlikely that you can do nearly as well as a professional.

5. For the activities where you need help, interview and hire professionals. You can hire them individually or ask your professional book advisor for suggestions of subcontractors they've already vetted.

6. Reach out to people who can help you. Your friends and other online connections can write reviews and post announcements of your book launch on social media. They may be able to introduce you to potential endorsers. Their initial purchases help create social proof that your book is worthwhile.

---

**MORAL** You do not have to self-publish all by yourself.

*Insert 11: Publication Activities*

1) Finish first draft. This includes several rounds of personal editing.
2) Send the draft to several beta readers, telling them how to give you feedback.
3) Receive the beta reader feedback and make updates to the draft.
4) Write front/back material such as dedication, about the author, acknowledgments.
5) Ask somebody well-known in your field to write a foreword.
6) Get the content and style of the book edited. It is a good idea to have somebody else do this to make sure your content is clear.
7) Create a cover design.
8) Create graphics for the book interior.
9) Format the book interior.
10) Request endorsements. Incorporate them into the cover design and book interior.
11) Create a launch plan.
12) Proofread.
13) Format the book for Kindle.
14) Acquire ISBNs.
15) Upload book components to publication services such as Amazon and Ingram.
16) Choose categories and write online sales information.
17) Line up people willing to buy the book on launch day and write reviews.
18) Launch. Then celebrate.
19) Find chances to talk and write about your book to keep it in people's minds.
20) Thank the people who have helped you.

# Chapter 15

# **Share Experiments: Network**

When you publish a book or article, how do you help readers find it? That's when it's important to think of the people in your network who could lend a hand. Perhaps they can review your manuscript and suggest improvements. Perhaps they can pass the word on to their networks that your valuable writing exists and is helpful.

Let me share a message from Adam Grant, author of *Give and Take*. Asking people to help is not putting a burden on everyone you ask. Some may not respond, but others will welcome an opportunity to help. It gives them a chance to be generous and to express their values. Some may ask for you to reciprocate later, but that is okay, too. It gives you a chance to be generous back.

# Share Experiment 13: Invite Beta Reviewers

## STORY: GIVING A BOOK A TRIAL RUN

Jia Li was very happy with her book. She had been working on it for months. She believed she had good stories from her long experience, good concepts that she had often explained to clients, and good activities that her clients found valuable.

Her publication advisor talked her into getting a beta review. Jia Li sent a version of the book out to six people who were all similar to her ideal readers. Some were friends, some colleagues, some former clients. She asked them to read it as a whole and to let her know how well it worked.

Some of her readers told her the book was absolutely needed by people like them. They wanted to know when they could send copies to friends. Some of the comments about what people liked were so strong that Jia Li asked reviewers if she could use them as endorsements of the book.

But some of the comments stung. More than half of the beta reviewers had trouble following the chapter order. Some felt the ideas were not totally clear. Some said they could not understand how to do the exercises. The exercises had always worked well with clients, but then, Jia Li would not be able to go with her book to explain them to new readers.

At first, Jia Li felt like giving up. Then, with the help of a good editor, she made some major adjustments to the order and filled in gaps that reviewers identified.

## OBSERVATION

When I was a software engineer, we were reminded over and over that the cost of fixing a bug goes up steeply after a product is released. In fact, the earlier you catch a bug, the better. It's better to find it in design than in internal testing. At the very latest, find it with customers willing to work with a beta product. After formal release, the costs include loss of customer confidence in the software product.

A software beta test is a trial in the final stages of development carried out by parties not involved in its development. Beta testers tend to try things that the developers didn't think about. They test assumptions. They get confused by the user interface. Beta testers are customers who agree to report problems in exchange for getting the product early.

Similarly, beta reviewers are fresh eyes on your book, seeing it without your preconceptions. Do they want to read it to the end? Do they find the organization clear? Do they find any mannerisms irritating? Do they feel something major is missing? All of this feedback is good to get and handle before the book goes to a professional editor.

Remember that humans tend to suffer from the negativity bias, which means that negative comments tend to have a more powerful impact than positive comments. You can manage this bias by making sure to spend at least as much time thinking about the positive comments as you do addressing the criticisms.

---
## STEPS
---

1. Identify people to invite to be beta readers for your book. Don't ask anyone who would worry about hurting your feelings. If you do not have appropriate people in mind, try looking online for people who offer beta reader services. Most of these steps assume you are asking people in your own network who will do it as a good will gesture and with a desire to support you.

2. Figure out how many beta reviewers you want. In my opinion, four or five is a good number. If you get too many, you may find yourself overwhelmed by feedback.

3. Invite twice that number to be reviewers. Take time with the invitation. Make it clear what you want and what you don't want. Tell them how much you would appreciate their feedback. Perhaps tell them you'll send a free copy of the book when it is available.

4. If you get more volunteers than you need, select the ones that best match your target audience. Consider diversity of age, geography, gender, and ethnicity. Thank the others and remind them that there will be opportunities later to help you with the book launch.

5. Ask your beta readers to let you know if their ability to meet the commitment changes.

6. Your editor or publishing advisor may have email templates for recruiting beta readers and/or giving them instructions.

7. Watermark the document so that it is clear that it is not to be shared. Word, for example, allows you to set a watermark.

8. Print the document to give to nearby reviewers or send it online. I prefer PDF format because nearly everybody can read it, and it discourages beta readers from marking up the document. Personally, I do not want beta readers trying to fix the problems they find. On the other hand, you might welcome their fixes.

9. Make sure you include page numbers, and consider having line numbers to make it easy to identify the locations of difficulties precisely.

10. Be clear what you do and do not want. Following is a little snippet from the email I sent to my beta reviewers.

*Insert 12: Section from an Email to Beta Readers*

What it means to be a beta reader:
- Read through the whole book with an eye on how well it works as a whole.
- Make comments at the book level -- whether the organization works, whether the order works, any topics that seem excessive or lacking or duplicative.
- Point out passages that aren't clear.

What it does not mean:
- Looking for grammatical errors or ill-constructed sentences or misspelled words.
- Doing any revising.
- Marking up the document.

I will have a content editor and a proofreader after the beta reviews are over.

I want to know if the pieces fit together in a way that people like you would find helpful. Please tell me what you find strong as well as what you find problematic. I promise to have a thick skin when I work through your comments.

11. Optionally create a template for the review that helps people focus their attention. I have included the template I sent my beta reviewers in Table 7.

12. Give your beta readers a deadline, and then nudge them as the deadline approaches.

13. Welcome their comments. Look for commonalities. Clarify stated concerns.

14. As you work through the beta comments, start each editing session by reviewing the positive comments. This will counter the tendency to focus on the negative, and it will remind you what NOT to change.

*Table 7: Sample Beta Review Questions*

| To beta readers, thank you for your willingness to read this draft and share your insights.<br><br>Specifically, please look for: | |
|---|---|
| Clarity | Is the chapter content clear? Are there areas with too much information that confuses rather than clarifies? |
| Flow | Does the order of the chapters and information work for you? Can you follow it easily? Can you think of anything that would make it flow more smoothly? |
| Placement | What information would be better placed in a different chapter, section, or explained in a different order? |
| Missing Information | What else would you like to see included? What is missing that would make the book better? Are there areas too skimpy on content and explanation? |
| Use of story | Are there enough anecdotes included to keep your interest? Where do I need to add more? Where are there too many? |
| Cultural sensitivity | Does it show respect for cultural differences? |
| Overall experience | Does it make you feel energized to write? |

**MORAL** Put on your rhinoceros hide. Valuable comments may sting.

# Share Experiment 14:
# Establish Your Expertise in Your Author Bio

## STORY: WHO AM I TO WRITE THIS BOOK?

Jermaine was stumped. She had written 50,000 words about a topic dear to her heart, but she could not seem to get herself to write the author bio for her book. It made her feel queasy.

Her writing coach suggested that she go to a bookstore, find an interesting topic, and pick up book after book just to read the author bio. Then she was to ask herself, "Am I more or less likely to buy the book, based on what I just read?"

She realized that sometimes she'd pick up an interesting title but think, "Who is this person, to write this topic? What do they know? Why should I care what they say?" The best bios made her see that the author had expertise she could trust.

Looking through the books reminded Jermaine that publishing her book meant asking people to spend time and money to access her writing. The sole job of her author statement was to convince them that she had the expertise to justify the expense.

Some of the bios seemed to go on and on, and she found herself wondering, "Why do I need to know that?" Others were so flat and uninformative that it was hard to keep her eyes on them. The best had just enough information about the author's expertise while still being short, interesting, and a pleasure to read.

## OBSERVATIONS

Some of the best advice I ever got about public speaking was to remind myself before every speech to shift my focus from myself ("How am I doing? Have I captured their attention? Am I smiling enough?") to the audience ("Do they see what I mean? Am I speaking about something that matters to them?"). Whenever I remember to do that, my nervousness turns into excitement.

The same shift helps when writing an author bio. One clue that you are too focused on yourself is asking yourself questions such as "Have I said the right things? Do I sound conceited? Why does it feel so icky to write about myself?" When you focus on potential readers, your internal questions sound more like, "What do they need to know about me to trust what I am telling them? What will help them see that I have knowledge and experience that make my words worth reading?"

Remember too that your bio is a small writing sample, like a tapas serving of your book. They may be sampling many books to decide which to buy. If your bio is clear, concise, easy to read, and answers their unspoken questions, they will feel their time has been respected. That may help them decide to spend more time reading your words.

## STEPS

1. This might be a good time to do or review Share Experiment 1 in Chapter 12 about picturing your ideal reader. This can help you switch focus from yourself to your readers.

2. Consider the questions your ideal reader may want answered. Here are some possibilities:

   - Does this author know the material? What education or experience underlies the author's expertise?

   - What gives this person a unique angle on the material? What makes their point of view different from others writing on the subject?

   - What will it be like to read this person's writing? Will it be fun, annoying, stimulating, confusing, inspiring?

3. Make a list of facts that you might want to bring up.

4. Read some author bios in books on your own shelves or on social media platforms such as LinkedIn. Which do you find easy and pleasant to read? What words do they use that you might include in your bio? Think about the questions they answer and how they position themselves. What could you adapt for your purposes?

5. Draft a bio that answers the questions you think your reader will care about. Don't worry too much about length. Keeping it short will come in the editing phase.

6. Write in the third person. He/she language will feel less like bragging than I language.

7. For everything that feels like bragging, doublecheck that it answers a question your reader might have. You do need to establish your expertise.

8. Numbers are good, particularly if they show a depth of expertise. For example, "I have coached thousands of school children," or "I have run 1500 writers' workshops."

9. Edit firmly. Some author bios, such as the one on the back cover, need to be very short. Think 60 to 90 words, maximum 150. If you have two answers to the same question, consider whether the second adds enough new information to be worth including. Check every *and* to see if you can compress.

10. Keep the outtakes. They will come in handy for other purposes, such as the author page inside your book or on your book website. I have short, medium, and long bios. I use them as starting points, but then tailor them for particular purposes. For example, if I am a podcast guest, I might mention other podcasts in which I have spoken.

11. Get someone who understands your target audience to give you honest feedback. How does your bio draft come across?

12. If you are completely stalled, get together with a friend who also needs a bio. Swap fact lists and write the first draft of each other's bios. You might be able to give each other a head start this way.

---

**MORAL** Keep your eyes on what the reader needs to know about you.

# Share Experiment 15:
# Gather Social Proof via Endorsements and Reviews

## STORY: THE ANSWER MAY BE YES

Jacinta was writing the book that she had sought in vain while going through a major crisis at work. Along the way, she spoke to many people who wanted to know when the book would come out. Some asked for advanced reader copies (ARCs) for themselves or for friends. After she had turned the draft over to an editor, her book advisor asked her, "Who are you going to ask for endorsements?"

That brought a whole host of unpleasant emotions to the surface. Her mind chatter sounded like: "Who am I to ask for their time? Why would they want to do this? What if they say no? Won't I be bothering them?"

Her book advisor had seen this before. "Just ask. Remember, not asking is equivalent to getting a no answer. If you ask, there's a chance you'll get a yes."

Fortunately, Jacinta had the list of people who had asked for ARCs. She picked out twelve that were most likely to be known to readers of her subject matter and/or most likely to say something cool. Jacinta drafted short personal emails, reminding them how they knew her and explaining why she thought they might be interested in her book. She attached a PDF of the current draft. She read each email several times before taking a deep breath and pushing send.

Six people responded right away. With just one nudge, they all sent in their endorsement paragraphs almost on time. A week later, a seventh paragraph arrived from someone who had not responded at all. He had been in the hospital and was only just catching up on his email.

## OBSERVATIONS

Most people need some kind of social proof that a book is good before they decide to buy it. They might pick up a book from a library shelf just on a whim, but spending money is another matter. Even the most prominent and well-known authors gather endorsements to demonstrate that their books are worthy. Some of these short statements are printed on the back cover of the book. An especially stellar one might appear on the front. Others go inside the book. Insert 13 shows one of my favorite book endorsements.

*Insert 13: Sample Endorsement*

> "This is one of the best books in all of positive psychology. It takes one of the most important areas of research – the character strengths – and makes it as accessible, as practical, and as inspiring as could be. I particularly love that it is written for sharing. Every couple and every family should have a copy. This will become my standard dinner party gift instead of a bottle of wine."
> ~ Jonathan Haidt, author of *The Righteous Mind* and *The Happiness Hypothesis*

Even people who do not know Jon Haidt can see that he has published two books of his own, which gives him credibility, and that he strongly approves of this book. His endorsement is only 70 words long.

Book reviews are another source of social proof. They range from articles published by online services, print journals, or newspapers to paragraphs posted by readers on a platform such as Amazon and Goodreads. For review articles, you can invite someone you respect to review it or submit your manuscript to a particular publication that runs reviews. *Library Journal* runs reviews of books that they consider of national interest that are readily available from national distributors. They must receive a PDF or ARC of the book at least three months before the month of publication. Other publications may have similar restrictions, so plan ahead. Kirkus allows self-publishers to purchase reviews. Acquisitions librarians often use Library Journal and Kirkus to make book buying decisions. Paid reviews are less credible than ones that people publish because they like the book, but the Kirkus service gains credibility because they do not guarantee positive reviews.

**STEPS**

1. Think about your plan for creating social proof. Make lists of people who might write endorsements, longer review articles, or Amazon reviews.

2. For some of your endorsements, think big. Who is a leader in the subject area of your book? Do you know that person? If not, do you know anybody who knows anybody who might know that person? Start thinking about how to build a relationship. Follow them on social media. Keep your eyes open for ways you can serve them.

3. For other endorsements, select people who are like your ideal readers.

4. When you ask, send sample endorsements that they could tailor and return to you. Some people will prefer to write their own, but others will be happy to have a first draft to alter.

5. Once you get your first endorsement, leverage it to get more. Even endorsers respond to social proof.

6. Think about the places your readers are likely to look for interesting books. That's where you want reviews to appear. Figure out how to submit a request for a review and when it needs to be received. Work that into your plan.

7. As soon as your book is available online, ask your beta readers and other supporters to post reviews on Amazon, Goodreads, or other services. If they got early copies, ask them to make that clear. Ideally, you would like to have 5 to 10 reviews posted by your official launch date.

8. When anybody tells you they like your book, ask them to write an online review. The number of Amazon reviews matters. It affects

the likelihood of your book showing up in searches and in lists of similar books.

9. Say thank you to everybody who helps you build social proof. Ask them to pass the word on to their friends.

---

**MORAL** Many people welcome opportunities to help others reach their dreams.

# Share Experiment 16: Spread the Word

## STORY: THE DREADED AUTHOR PLATFORM

Justus wrote a book of beautiful essays. His book combined hard-headed practicality and poetry. A friend introduced him to a publisher's representative, who loved the book. But when it came to publishing it, the representative said Justus would need at least 10,000 names on his email and social media lists before the publisher would talk to him seriously. After spending several months working on his list, Justus returned to the rep with new numbers. But they weren't enough. This time the publication company wanted 50,000 names.

Justus decided against finding a publisher. The representative was telling him that although he loved the book himself, he could not see a way that the publishing house would make money from it. Justus published it himself and used his improved list to announce the publication. He also lined up friends and colleagues to get the word out to their friends and colleagues. He realized his was not the only email list that was important.

## OBSERVATIONS

An author's platform is essentially the author's network. That means people who know you by name, know something about your capabilities, and have shown interest in your work in the past.

That network may include people on your email list, social media followers, and blog readers. There are steps you can take to augment your platform. Generally, these steps require time and consistency.

Your own network is not the only network you can reach. If you have people who think highly of your work, you can ask them to inform their networks. You can help them help you.

**STEPS**

1. Take inventory of your author platform right now. Do you have an email list? Do you have social media followers? Do you have friends who might reach out to their friends?

2. Take steps to build your platform. There are many ideas out there that will carry you further. Here are some suggestions:

   - Post regularly in a blog. Use interesting keywords, and look into search engine optimization so that your words are found. Keep your blog active so that it shows up in searches.

   - Think about where your target readers are likely to hang out. What other blogs might they read? What social media might they follow? Try to be there with comments and appreciation.

   - Post little tidbits of your content regularly on a social media platform such as Instagram or Twitter.

   - Build a website that represents what you offer to the world.

   - Write and publish on other sites, such as popular blogs and other publications in your niche.

   - Look for podcasters who might want to interview you.

   - Start your own podcast on the subject.

3. As you prepare to publish, work out a series of emails for various audiences to let them know your book is coming. If you are working with a book advisor or publisher, they may have templates to help you write these emails.

4. Identify friends who would be willing to support your launch. Make it as easy as possible by providing sample copy and dates for posting. Support them by liking their posts. Say thank you.

5. On your website, have a page that offers a free gift related to your book that you give readers in exchange for their email addresses. This is a way to expand your platform. Be sure to promise not to share their email address.

6. Occasionally send your platform news of your book. Always say thank you.

7. Keep going, even after your book is launched. A launch gives early momentum, but it is up to you to recognize opportunities to keep spreading the word. Write more blog posts, post more social media tidbits, and share links to the reviews you requested in Share Experiment 15 earlier in this chapter.

8. Consider hiring a public relations firm that will get you TV interviews and other chances to talk about your book.

**MORAL** Use your network and connected networks to reach readers.

*Table 8: Collected Morals from the Share Experiments*

| Share # | Category | Moral |
|---------|----------|-------|
| Share 1 | Audience | Imagine advisors who can speak for your ideal audience. |
| Share 2 | Audience | Some ideas are like wall studs, supportive but not needing to show. |
| Share 3 | Audience | Cultural sensitivity broadens your audience. |
| Share 4 | Support | It is easier to be accountable to someone else than to yourself. |
| Share 5 | Support | Spell out an agreement today to prevent future heartache. |
| Share 6 | Support | Seek a writers' group that can give balanced feedback. |
| Share 7 | Support | A structured review works better than a free-for-all. |
| Share 8 | Publish | There is more than one way to become a published author. |
| Share 9 | Publish | With persistence, it is possible to make money writing. |
| Share 10 | Publish | Find the route to readers that works for you. |
| Share 11 | Publish | You can outsource some work to a literary agent or publisher. |
| Share 12 | Publish | You do not have to self-publish all by yourself. |
| Share 13 | Network | Put on your rhinoceros hide. Valuable comments may sting. |
| Share 14 | Network | Keep your eyes on what the reader needs to know about you. |
| Share 15 | Network | Many people welcome opportunities to help others reach their dreams. |
| Share 16 | Network | Use your network and connected networks to reach readers. |

# Chapter 16

# Moving From Share Back to Write

You have let other people help you, and you have launched your words out into the world. For a quick review, the morals for the Share experiments are listed together in Table 8.

Reflect on what you have learned by sharing your writing with friends, colleagues, and strangers. How have your ideas been changed by their feedback? What skills served you well, and what skills do you want to enhance? What would you do differently next time?

Once a piece has been published, it is probably time to start on your next writing project. That might be another book, or it might be articles that draw attention to your book with the goal of making it a bestseller.

You could go back to the Sit experiments to see if there are any ways to bolster your confidence or refine your habits. Or you could return directly to the Write experiments to imagine, draft, and edit something new.

Welcome to the world of writing.

# Conclusion

One day it finally sank in for me. The first draft does not have to be any good. I just need it as a jumping off point for playing with ideas and words. Writing became much easier. Then it became fun.

Writing has enriched my life. It has resulted in fruitful partnerships producing books, articles, and book chapters. It has allowed me to reach people around the world with my own particular ideas about human well-being. It has surrounded me with a community of writers who are also seeking to make a positive difference. I have influenced many more books than I have written. I read with greater awareness because I write. I capture family events so that my family does not forget. I create memory joggers for my future self. I wish these benefits for you and more.

I have had tremendous fun pulling this book together. I relived the creative ways my clients and I got around various stumbling blocks and opened our minds to inspiration. I remembered what keeps us going.

As I close, let me remind you that we are already writers. Writing is like any craft. It gets better with deliberate practice and paying attention. I never stop practicing.

The experiments in this book are ways to practice the craft. The Sit experiments show how to settle our minds to the task and build habits that return us to writing frequently. The Write experiments show how to imagine what we want to say, draft powerful messages, and then edit rough drafts until they are clear and a pleasure to read. The Share experiments show how to find support from other people and then put our words out there for strangers to see.

How can you make this book work for you? Different writers are working on different skills. Even the same person may focus on different skills at different times. I invite you to make this book your personal manual for getting better at the craft of writing. Select an experiment that seems to address the skill you want to build or the obstacle you want to get past. Try it out. Adjust it as needed to fit your own writing needs. One writer complained that the first step in a particular experiment made her feel discouraged. I suggested that she just cross it out in her copy of the book.

Keep notes on your adjustments. Then step back and evaluate. Was that experiment the right approach for you? If so, keep practicing. If not, set it aside guilt-free. This is your practice and your manual. As you keep experimenting, incorporate what works into your craft.

You are a writer. Let the world see the words you weave together.

# Acknowledgments

So many people contributed to the quality of this book that I am almost afraid to name them for fear I will leave someone out.

Members of the Theano Writers' Workshops reviewed early drafts of individual experiments and helped the book take shape. Thank you, Nancy Ancowitz, Jodi Atkinson, Andrew Brady, Brian Branagan, Aren Cohen, Nil Demircubuk, Sid Efromovich, Sherri Fisher, Andrea Goulet, Carol Grannis, Natalie Griffin, Anil Kale, Helen Kaye, Bess Keller, Jan Irene Miller, Kathi Norman, Ejemen Okojie, Leora Rifkin, Lindsay Shea, Yashi Srivastava, Jan Stanley, Margarita Tarragona, Darrin Tulley, Karen Warner, and Kim Wimmer. Your words were clear and helpful. You never discouraged me. You gave me many suggestions for making the book better.

I thank my beta readers who read the book when it was almost complete. I say almost complete because their suggestions inspired me to add the summaries at the end of each major section, revise stories, and add steps that made the experiments even better. Thank you all for your time, attention, and kindness: Aren Cohen, Andrea Goulet, Ejemen Okojie, Joanne Schaefer, Andrew Soren, and Corey Zadik.

Diana Needham of Business Book Partners helped me navigate the shoals of professionally publishing a book. She was the model of the general contractor idea in Share Experiment 12. She recommended the book editor, Nanette Levin, who masterfully found and fixed the rough spots that I could no longer see.

Jane E. Scott and I grew up together. Our mothers were friends for more than 80 years, and we hope to exceed their record. I thank her for the grace and humor of the foreword.

Susannah helped me understand freelance writing. I omit her last name at her request. She was generous with her time. She shared her experience thoughtfully and helped me understand details that must have seemed basic to her.

Dori and Kate Sears were delighted to have me share the words of their grandmother, Sally Bryan. They responded, "We're thrilled that you found our grandma's words helpful and are more than happy to have you share her 'pearls of wisdom' (as we always called them!) with the world. We loved helping Grandma make her *Book of S*, and we still treasure it."

I thank Jan Stanley and Conrad Macalalad for giving me the courage to start my first writers' workshops in 2013. I also appreciate Richard Gabriel for writing about a workshop process that could have arisen from positive psychology. He showed me the way.

Over the years, I have asked writers many times what helped them make progress. I have quoted 14 of them in this book. Their names appear in the credits, but I want to thank them collectively for their wisdom and generosity.

Once upon a time, I helped my close friend, Karen Long, finish her master's thesis and my husband, Edward Britton, finish his dissertation. Those might be my earliest experiences helping someone else write. My husband and I together helped our long-suffering children, Laura and Thomas, learn how to write, and our daughter inspired at least one of the stories. I thank all of them for their unwavering support.

# Resources

When I started writing this book, I used this section as the dumping ground for every interesting resource I found working out my experiments. Some entries were popular books written by psychologists about what they found studying habits, intentions, inspiration, and other relevant mental states. Others were how-to articles about freelancing, blogging, publishing, writing book proposals, and spreading the word about a book.

What most had in common was that you can find them or links to buy them on the Internet.

That is strike one against including them in the book itself. Who wants to type out URLs printed in a book in order to find Web resources?

Strike two is that I am not sure about all of them. Perhaps as I look further, I will find an even better resource. This is a dynamic space.

Strike three is that the list keeps growing. There are wonderful things out there written about writing and publishing.

That is why all I am going to give you here is one resource, a link to the page on the book's website where I provide an organized and annotated bibliography of resources. That way I can keep updating it. When you use it, you can click on links to go right to the sources you want to access.

https://SitWriteShare.com/Resources

# Credits

# Selected Publications

Details about these publications, including co-authors, co-editors, and links to access, appear in the book's resources.

## Co-authored Books

*Thriving Women, Thriving World: An Invitation to Dialogue, Healing, and Inspired Actions.*

*Smarts and Stamina: The Busy Person's Guide to Optimal Health and Performance*

## Books of Collected Articles from Positive Psychology News

*Resilience: How to Navigate Life's Curves*
*Gratitude: How to Appreciate Life's Gifts*
*Character Strengths Matter: How to Live a Full Life*

## Co-Authored Chapters in Books

Acting "As If" in Executive Coaching. In *Positive Psychiatry: A Casebook.*

Positive Psychology for Sports Leaders. In *Positive Psychology in Sport and Physical Activity*

## Primary Papers

Increasing Job Satisfaction: Coaching with Evidence-based Interventions

Specifying Software Requirements for Complex Systems: New Techniques and Their Application

# About the Author

Kathryn Britton didn't start her career intending to focus on writing. After an undergraduate degree in English, she followed her interests into a computer science career with the Naval Research Laboratory and IBM. She was surprised to find herself writing more prose than code as she delivered specifications, design documents, and papers. Her first publication, a 1980 paper about specifying software requirements, was reprinted in a 2001 book and is still cited. As an IBM Master Inventor, she mentored many people writing invention disclosures.

In 2006, Kathryn earned a Master of Applied Positive Psychology (MAPP) degree at the University of Pennsylvania. A search for a new career to contribute to world-wide well-being led her to coaching and helping people write. Since 2007, she has edited more than 1500 articles for the online news source, *Positive Psychology News,* helping many people start their publication careers. Every article taught her something about reaching an online audience.

In 2013, she ran her first writers' workshop using an approach learned at IBM. Since then, she has conducted more than 1500 workshop sessions reviewing more than 3000 pieces of writing. She also coaches individual authors drafting books, dissertations, blogs, academic papers, and articles for online magazines. Twelve books have emerged from writers' workshops, and more are underway.

Kathryn continues to write herself. She has published more than 100 articles online in *Positive Psychology News*, *Forbes*, and *LinkedIn*. She has been the co-editor of three books and the co-author of two others. *Sit Write Share* is her first solo effort as a book author. She follows her own lead. Every experiment in *Sit Write Share* was reviewed in at least one workshop.

Kathryn reached this point in her career through detours and discovery. She understands the challenges writers face. Sometimes there are so many ideas that it is hard to focus. Sometimes the words won't come. Sometimes it is hard to decide on a particular audience. That's why she founded Theano Coaching LLC, to get individual writers unstuck and enable workshop participants to help each other make progress.

*Sit Write Share* is Kathryn's chance to share what she learned along the way. It's your chance to benefit from unusual perspectives she gained from multiple careers in very different disciplines. Writing has been key to all of them.

www.ingramcontent.com/pod-product-compliance
Lightning Source LLC
Chambersburg PA
CBHW071200210326
41597CB00016B/1621